# PULSE Conversations for Change

## Dr. Nancy Love, PhD

Published by **The PULSE Institute Inc.**

REPRODUCTION AND USE POLICY CONCERNING THIS MATERIAL:

Any **PULSE** materials, including the Book, Participant's Workbook, and associated PowerPoint presentation and slides, whether in printed or electronic form, are the intellectual property of Nancy Love of **The PULSE Institute Inc.** and represent the investment of years of research, design, and development. We appreciate your use of this material, and request that you respect our investment in its creation by acting in accordance with the following restrictions:

Reproduction by any means, physical or electronic, of any part of the program materials or their components may be made only with the express written permission of **The PULSE Institute Inc.** Any permitted print reproductions must show the following statement on each page (without quotes):

"Copyright 2008 by Nancy Love of **The PULSE Institute Inc.**, www.pulseinstitute.com Reproduced by permission"

Related Services:
For information about customized in-house training, public registration seminars, speeches, conference presentations, or consulting on the **PULSE** Conversation Programs please contact:

The PULSE Institute Inc.
Nancy Love, PhD
Phone: 888-882-8804
Web Page: www.pulseinstitute.com

# TABLE OF CONTENTS

Travel quotes which appear throughout are from the *Old World Journal.*

"When you travel you discover as much about yourself as you do about the world."

Dr. Nancy Love, PhD

"We are linguistically constructed, relational selves"

*A Positive Revolution in Change,* Cooperrider and Whitney, p. 3, 1999, www.appreciativeinquiry.org

# Chapter 1: Prepare for the Conversation

Thank you for joining me here in this book, on this adventure. Have you ever read a book about conversation before? Whether you have or you haven't, let me take this opportunity to explain to you more about this particular book on conversation in this first chapter, the *Prepare* chapter. Once I have explained the purpose of the book, the process that it follows, the protocol that is used and discussed authority, confidentiality and time, then you can decide whether or not you would like to continue to read on and learn more about the story of PULSE in Chapter 2, what makes PULSE different in Chapter 3, applications for PULSE in Chapter 4 and the call to action in Chapter 5.

The purpose of the book is to acquaint you with the PULSE conversation and to pique your interest in learning more about what it is, why it is important and how it can be applied to conversations that you have every day. Improving the quality of conversations is the goal because improved conversations result in improved relationships and families and organizations. All of us belong to one of those and all of us at some point have had conversations that were less then satisfying or less than satisfactory. Once you become aware of the PULSE frame for conversations and the PULSE principles that underlie the frame you become what we call a PULSE Practitioner - someone who uses the frame to structure conversations or events or even ideas for writing.

I have written this book for past, present and future PULSE practitioners. If you know about PULSE, this book will deepen your understanding of the frame and its applications. If you are presently learning about PULSE, this book will add to your understanding of the process and its principles. If you are new to PULSE, this book provides the basic understanding that will allow you to practice, to become a PULSE practitioner. If you are a mediator, facilitator, human resources professional, social worker, teacher, professional or leader of any kind, the PULSE frame will help you in your work. If you are none of those, PULSE will help you speak and listen to others differently so that you will have more satisfying and effective conversations. PULSE works to frame difficult, dangerous, crucial, critical, and everyday conversations. However you use it or wherever you are on your PULSE journey, there is something in this book to take you a little further, to guide you a little closer to the Content, Process and Response that make up the PULSE frame.

The book is intended to be conversational, too. Because you are not with me as I write I will make assumptions about what you might say as a result of what I have said and I will attempt to anticipate questions or concerns you have as we go along. Know that as a reader you have an open invitation to continue this dialogue, this learning conversation, with me at any time. Just call or write. I also invite you to read it more than once and notice how you move further along the PULSE conversation road with each reading. *PULSE Conversations for Change*, like the PULSE frame is simple yet complex. Look for the layers and enjoy the exploration.

I am writing in a new travel journal that I bought at an airport. The journal has quotes from different authors and celebrities about travel at the top of certain pages throughout the book.  At the top of this page is a quote from Amelia Earhart, a heroine of mine.  "Adventure is worthwhile," she says and I agree.  Adventure is worthwhile and this is the beginning of an adventure for me.  It is exciting and wonderful and humbling all at the same time.  I am happy to have Amelia Earhart as a travel companion.  Another female aviator, Nancy Harkness Love, came to my attention years ago when friends bought me a tee shirt with a picture of the other Nancy Love in the cock pit of her World War II cargo plane.  Hers was a great story.  I was immediately proud to share her name.  Her courage and commitment to making a difference in her world inspired me to be courageous and committed in mine.  Amelia Earhart also has a wonderful name that incorporates words like ear and hart.  Listening with HEART is one of the principles that I intend to write about in this book. I wonder if it is coincidental that I choose this blank travel journal to begin the writing of *PULSE Conversations for Change*.  Coincidence or not, I am happy to have the aviators along.  Most of the writing has been done on airplanes and in airports.  The significance is not lost on me.

In fact there are many adventurers on this journey with me.  I have just spent two wonderful weeks hosting a PULSE Train the Trainer event in the Rocky Mountains.  Over those two weeks twenty people joined me to consider the PULSE conversation frame, its simple beauty and its complex strength and as we thought together in rich dialogue, deeply listening and thinking even more deeply, the deliberate action, the logical next step emerged.  Write the book... and so I did.

The audience for this book is you if you believe that there is a better way to have conversations, if you expect that quality conversations lead to quality relationships, if you assume that a structure and skills for conversations might improve your success, if you are at all concerned about your own ability to have productive conversations and if you hope that there is a way to help others or coach others to have successful conversations. If these are your criteria for a great and useful book then you have come to the right place. You have no doubt witnessed conversations that were difficult, tense and intense. You have also no doubt watched a skilled conversationalist rescue the conversations from the brink of disaster through a simple change in focus or using a different word or asking a question. This book is aimed at building understanding and practical tools, revealing the art and the science of conversation, so that you can become the kind of conversationalist, or as we say, PULSE practitioner, who can skillfully and deliberately manage a conversation to mutually agreeable resolution.

The book is written for those who think, for those who do and for those who feel. Everyone does all three but as humans we have a predisposition or tendency to be more comfortable thinking, doing, or feeling. As you read, notice where you are more comfortable. Reading of course will appeal immediately to the thinkers. Reading about the *content* or theory of PULSE will appeal to the thinkers. Reading about the *process* of PULSE will appeal to the doers. Reading about the *response* in PULSE will appeal to the emoters or feelers. The content, process, response theme, PULSE's "CPR", runs throughout the book. It is one of the ways that you *experience* PULSE in the book as well as read about it. This is what I will call experiential reading, which is like experiential learning, only you do it on your own. I wrote the book using the PULSE frame as an organizer for my thoughts, much the way I did when I wrote my dissertation on Accountability and Change. Each chapter is named after a piece of the frame: Prepare, Uncover, Learn, Search and Explain. The intention of each piece in the frame is matched in the chapters that follow. So as you read and become familiar with the content, process and response of PULSE, you will also experience the PULSE frame in the structure of the conversation between you and me, as reader and writer.

Prepare for the Conversation
Uncover the Circumstance
Learn the Significance
Search the Possibilities
Explain the Plan

A friend of mine describes the PULSE frame as an archetype for conversations because although it is unique it is also universal. Listen to any structured conversation and notice how it includes the PULSE frame. Any planning tool will predictably include a version of the PULSE frame. PULSE is a discovery of how good, effective conversations occur.

Conversations are the means that we use to structure and interpret our world. They are significant and vital for relationships and organizations. Having studied conversations I have found that effective, successful and satisfying conversations contain five elements or pieces that are described in detail throughout this book. PREPARE, UNCOVER, LEARN, SEARCH, EXPLAIN.

You will notice that the acronym for the five elements of the conversation spell PULSE and so you will find that this kind of effective, successful and satisfying conversation is referred to as the PULSE conversation. Because the book also follows the frame for the conversation you will also experience PULSE as you read about it. At present you are in *Prepare*, the chapter that is intended to prepare you for the rest of the book.

## Purpose

The purpose of the book is to acquaint you with PULSE (Prepare, Uncover, Learn, Search, Explain) so that you can use it to effectively guide your own conversations if you so choose. The purpose is also to provide a firm base for understanding not just what to do in the PULSE frame but also why it works and how it makes people feel. Descriptions of the content, process and response related to PULSE are included. Ultimately, at the end of the book there will be a *call to action* for you to hear and acknowledge or ignore. In fact you and only you will decide how to use this book and for what purpose. Suggestions are made and they are only suggestions based on the experiences of others, who like yourself, were looking for a new approach to conversation, to difficult situations, that would improve their ability to adapt and deal with conflict and build relationships in their world.

## Process

The *Prepare* chapter that you are reading now outlines the means by which this learning conversation will be structured and guided.  It will answer the question "*How* will this conversation proceed?"  Once *Prepare* is complete Chapter 2, *Uncover*, will uncover the circumstances of the conversation, what you and I are here to share, the topic of our learning conversation. In this chapter I will share with you the mystery of PULSE, the evolution that lead to the discovery of the frame for Conversations for Change and I will describe what influences have played a role in the discovery. Chapter 2 uncovers the PULSE story from my own perspective and from the perspective of participants in workshops and conversations.  Although you are not physically present, I will include other points of view so that both sides of the PULSE story are presented.

In Chapter 3, *Learn*, I will share with you the meaning, the significance of the PULSE frame. We can explore together the unique and common characteristics of the frame.  The purpose of Chapter 3 is to answer the question "*Why*  is PULSE important, what makes it the same as or different from other conversation frames?" I will outline the beliefs, expectations, assumptions, concerns, and hopes that contribute to the criteria that give the PULSE frame its strength.  Once the criteria are clear, we can search the possible applications of the PULSE Conversation for Change in Chapter 4, *Search*.  Applications in writing, teaching, negotiation, mediation, project and change management, leadership and Appreciative Inquiry will be explored.

In Chapter 5, *Explain*, I will suggest a plan of action or a call to action for your role and mine in the future of the PULSE Conversation for Change.

## Protocol

A new quote appears at the top of this page in the travel journal. Ralph Waldo Emerson writes "*Do not go where the path may lead: go instead where there is no path and leave a trail*." I am leaving a trail on a new path, a path which others have already begun to follow. One of the items we pack for the journey on the PULSE path is a common protocol that guides interactions. It is a way of speaking and listening to each other that allows for, no requires, inclusion and appreciation of self and others. It is a protocol that was developed more than 10 years ago and that has served me well. PULSE Practitioners, which is the term we use for people on this path, agree to speak *gently* with each other, to speak so that the other person can keep on listening, to choose our words carefully and thoughtfully so that the other person can hear them. We use 'gently' rather than 'respectfully' because sometimes out of respect people leave pieces of the truth out and that is often counterproductive. PULSE practitioners agree to speak *honestly* to each other, to say what we are thinking in a gentle way. PULSE practitioners agree to be *open* to hearing what the other person is saying and are willing to allow any new information, heard or experienced, to influence perceptions. PULSE practitioners agree to use examples and be *specific* because we understand that words create worlds and that shared meaning is important. Life experiences add different meanings to common words. You may be using the same word as me and attaching different meaning to it. You and I may be describing two different experiences with the same word. Clarity is important in conversation so using examples and being specific can alleviate or at least mitigate the confusion or misunderstanding between us. PULSE practitioners agree to *talk*, to say what they are thinking rather than just thinking it. We know that thinking, not talking can be explosive. We use the TNT acronym, Thinking Not Talking, to remind us of that. Thoughts, no matter how seemingly inconsequential, indicate a response to our environment and are better shared. In fact we know that if we do not say all that we are thinking we will not be psychologically prepared to move on, so PULSE practitioners agree to say what they are thinking in a gentle way so that the other person can keep on listening.

This Gentle, Honest, Open, Specific, Talk, or GHOST protocol has been a basic travel companion for PULSE practitioners for more than a decade. When it is used as a protocol for conversation, new possibilities for the future emerge as a result of this change in approach. This new way of speaking and listening to each other encourages full disclosure. People are invited to consider a different version of the story from the past, a new understanding of the impact in the present and a new vision of the future together. The acceptance of this protocol alone has transformed conversations and allowed parties to reach not only settlement of troublesome circumstances but sustainable resolutions and stronger relationships.

Given the importance of the GHOST protocol, as it is referred to by PULSE practitioners, my commitment to you, the reader, is to be gentle and honest, open and specific and to talk. I agree to say what I am thinking in a gentle way throughout this learning conversation and I agree to be open to hear what you have to say as is my habit with participants in the workshops, and I commit to allowing what you have to say to influence my perspective. I invite you to do the same. My invitation to you is to use the GHOST protocol to guide your own conversations beginning today, beginning now. Think of a conversation you had recently or are about to have. How will the GHOST protocol change your approach to the conversation? How will sharing the protocol with the other person before the conversation affect the possible outcomes of the conversation?

The GHOST protocol is modeled by the practitioner and is instrumental in setting the tone of the conversation. Knowing and accepting the protocol before a meeting begins allows people to relax and feel safe because they know how everyone is expected to behave and because of that expectation they will feel more amenable to open discussion and full disclosure. It is this openness that enables the full disclosure which is necessary for effective, successful conversation to occur and sustainable resolutions to emerge. Sometimes a simple suggestion to speak gently will be enough to change the interaction and the relationship.

## Authority

Another question that is asked in Prepare in the PULSE conversation is "Do you have the authority to resolve or decide things in this conversation?" The purpose of the question is to ensure that parties do not waste time talking about things that they cannot change and instead that they focus on what is within their control, their circle of influence.  If parties are unsure as to their level of authority then the practitioner may ask them to consider keeping the conversation focused on those things that are within their authority.  The question is revisited repeatedly throughout the conversation.  Parties need to be clear what is doable and feasible and within their authority for the resolutions that they choose to be sustainable.  Asking at the beginning tends to focus the conversation where it will be most helpful, in the future, on those topics that are a priority and are within the control of the parties.

In this conversation that you and I are sharing, your authority as a reader comes from curiosity, I am guessing.  You have chosen this book instead of others because of an interest in the topic or because someone has suggested it to you or for some other reason known only to you.  Whatever brought you to the reading qualifies you to engage in the reading and to make decisions about what you will do as a result of having read.

My authority as a writer has evolved from many years of study around leadership and conversation culminating in a PhD in Educational Research with a focus on leadership.  I wrote what I called an 'Appreciative Portraiture', a mixture of academic writing and poetic considerations of leaders leading change in their organizations.  As a result of the research I came to "know" leadership as *vicarious responsibility* and leaders as negotiators of perceptions of the past, present and future of change initiatives they are leading.  I have written about and studied leaders and mediation for the past decade or so, always focusing on language, dialogue and conversation as the medium through which they do their work. I have written workbooks and delivered workshops on leadership and mediation, communication and PULSE conversations over the past twenty years and have learned so much from participants and authors of other works and accept now that, as synthesizer of that knowledge, I have become an expert.

I will also draw on my own direct experience in this world for "author"ity. I have served as an educator and high school principal and as a mediator for many years. Through experiences as vested partner in leadership and learning conversations and as intervener in disputes and highly emotional situations, I have collected and become the living conversation that is PULSE. Opportunities to be engaged in learning conversations continue to 'inform and form' me as Margaret Wheatley would say. I am no stranger to responsibility and have accepted an awesome responsibility as it was thrust upon me throughout my life. My latest, emerging responsibility has become to share what I know about the PULSE conversation with others, like you, in this book.

My role, as author, has become clearer over the past five months as I began to see with new eyes the possibilities in PULSE. You will notice that I wrote the book from *I* and *we*. It is not the royal *we* but instead the collective *we* the Buddhist *we*, the inclusive *we*, the 'everyone-who-has-ever-influenced-my-thinking' *we*. Many people have shared, contributed, sometimes unknowingly, to the emerging PULSE frame. The "we" recognizes and acknowledges every one of those contributions. Many of you who are reading this now are among the contributors and I thank you for that. In some way, everyone in my world has contributed as I learned what to do and say and what not to do and say to have effective successful conversations ... even my ex-husbands and especially my current one have taught me the art and science of conversation through the opportunities they afforded me to practice.  A core belief for PULSE practitioners is inclusiveness.  You are all included in the *we* you see in this book.

## Confidentiality

My role is conduit, messenger, author of what we have often referred to as the 'un-secret' that is the discovery of the PULSE frame.  Sharing it with the world, with past, present and future PULSE practitioners, is the purpose of this book so to address the confidentiality question that comes at the beginning of every PULSE conversation, let me invite you to tell as many people as you see fit and I will do the same.  If anyone you know is interested in improving the quality of their conversations share the book or the information with them.  At PULSE our mission statement or as we call it Purpose Statement reads  "World peace one conversation at a time."

## Time

My intention is to have us spend five chapters together Each is written so that you can read it independent of the others.  It is written so that it can be used to create a jigsaw reading exercise Sections called Uncover, Learn1, Learn2 and Search are deliberate in length to allow people to share the reading.  What that means is that if sixteen people were divided into four groups and each group were assigned a reading they could take the time to read one of those sections and then come back together and share what they read with those who had read the same section.  Then they could share their reading and the wisdom of their group with a mixed group to get the essence of all of the readings.  In this way, it would take about ninety minutes to learn what is in this book through the dialogue of the jigsaw.

## Jig Saw Reading

| Uncover | Learn 1 | Learn 2 | Search |
|---------|---------|---------|--------|
| A1 | A2 | A3 | A4 |
| B1 | B2 | B3 | B4 |
| C1 | C2 | C3 | C4 |
| D1 | D2 | D3 | D4 |

- Ones read *Uncover*
- Twos read *Learn 1*
- Threes read *Learn 2*
- Fours read *Search*

1. Take 20 minutes to read your section.
2. Then meet with the people who also read your section and share with each other what you learned in the reading, identifying the salient points that you feel would be important to share with those who had not read your section.
3. Then, A's, B's, C's and D's meet, so that there is one person from each reading group in the new configuration. Each person shares their understanding from the reading and the like group meeting of their section.
4. Debrief the Content, the Process and the Response to Jigsaw Reading.

Ninety minutes is the time we ask participants to set aside for a PULSE conversation. Just setting the time aside is an indication of a willingness to step into the solution circle and work on the topic, become informed, have present knowledge affirmed and confirmed. It is a commitment of time where participants agree that no walking away or power plays will occur. This agreement serves to curb reflexes to the perceptions of threat that might be felt during the initial phases. These reflexes are commonly known as fight, flight or freeze. Accordingly, I would ask that you commit to reading the entire book, to staying in the process until you have experienced all of it. I will commit to being here whenever you pick up the book to read the next chapter or section. Let's agree on the time it takes to read the book in its entirety as the time we will spend together.

## Roles

My role as author or writer is to guide the conversation, to answer the questions as they are presented and to assume the questions that might be asked by you the reader and answer those in anticipation. I agree to stay engaged until I have answered all of the questions that you might have about how to lead successful PULSE conversations using the frame. Your role, as reader, is to stay engaged until a mutually satisfactory outcome has been reached. That could mean that you have learned what you have come to learn, that you have acquired the skills and knowledge to do what you need to do, that you have become a PULSE practitioner. You will define when you are satisfied and I will still be here if you need more answers.

# PULSE

"I travel a lot; I hate having my life disrupted by routine." Caskie Stinnett, who is unfamiliar to me, said that at the top of my writing page. It is true of me. I have never been tamed. Routine and I are acquaintances and I long occasionally for the safety and comfort of routine in my life. Like any old acquaintances meeting from time to time we soon run out of things to say to each other and it is time to move on to the next adventure. I do not confuse routine with structure because within a structure or a protocol there is lots of room for creativity, differentness and adventure. The protocol and structure of PULSE, rather than becoming routine, seems to release creativity within its safe environment. People go further with their ideas, travel more if you will, and become more adventuresome within this safe vessel.

Patricia Shaw talks about the habitual patterns of response that emerge in facilitated meetings and how the conversations that recreate them have the potential for evolving what she calls "novel forms of practice" (p.2, 2002). It is within the safe environment for inquiry that is PULSE that new ideas and new solutions emerge. No two conversations are alike. Each is unique and new and exciting, full of possibilities even within the structure of a frame. A frame like PULSE outlines the boundary of the event and focuses it on a subject for the art or for the conversation. It does not limit the possibilities within the frame for a changing story, changing perceptions and an outcome that may not be visible at the outset. To use a dramatic metaphor, although the stage is set for a peaceful productive conversation, there is a large measure of improvisation on the stage as each act

Dr. Nancy Love, PhD

unfolds and lots of room for creative expression within the frame.

By now you may be asking what is PULSE? What is this frame, this conversation for change? And why is it important to me? The answers are simple and yet complex. PULSE is People Using Language Skills Effectively. PULSE is Prepare, Uncover, Learn, Search, Explain. PULSE is conversations for change. PULSE is guiding questions and conversation flow maps. PULSE is a frame rather than a model because people build models while they look through frames. PULSE is about changing perceptions and reframing the world and our experiences in it in such a way as to focus on the appreciative aspects of what we see. Two dimensionally it looks like this:

*Figure 1: The PULSE Frame*

It represents the patterns that emerged as I studied effective conversations and how they were structured. Although I was not in search of an archetype for conversations, it seems that I may have found one. Effective conversations begin with a *prepare* stage. On the poster, the conversation leader or change agent represented by the △ talks to the parties, represented by the P's. The conversation leader or △ outlines the purpose, process, protocol and establishes authority, level of confidentiality, a time frame and introduces the role of the △ to guide the conversation and the P's to stay engaged until a mutually satisfactory plan of action is reached. In effective conversations the next thing that happens is that an agenda is set. Time is spent listening to each of the parties while they have a chance to individually tell their story so that they can *uncover* what they have come into the conversation to resolve or decide. In fact this section of the conversation is about the circumstances from the past. Next the parties speak directly to each other as they explore their underlying interests or motivation and answer the question, why is this circumstance important. Parties take the opportunity to *learn* from each other what is significant, what their beliefs and expectations, their assumptions, concerns and hopes are in the situation. They identify what's missing for them, sometimes with raised voices and in hurtful ways. What's missing, the reframed hurt and anger, form the criteria for resolution. The trick is to listen for the criteria and articulate them into underlying motivations. Once identified these reframes serve as criteria for the next stage where parties *search* for possibilities in a brainstorming session where new ideas are generated first and then evaluated. Parties search for options for moving forward together, evaluate them against the criteria and then they *explain* in writing a plan of action so that the future they have described together can be implemented and sustained. Prepare, Uncover, Learn, Search, Explain...PULSE.

As I studied conversations I noticed that the elements were always present when outcomes were sustainable and effective. They were not necessarily done in a lock step way or with any kind of deliberateness. It was just the way the conversation evolved. Sometimes the protocol was understood. Often the agenda was sent out ahead of time. Sometimes the dialogue was ferocious and the conversation ended without resolution only to resume when calmer heads prevailed with suggestions for moving forward and action planning. The successful, effective conversations always included the five elements. PULSE represents a pattern that emerged in successful conversations even when circumstances were difficult or seemingly impossible.

Within the frame of the conversations that I observed there was a notion of moving from the past circumstance in Uncover to the present significance in Learn to the future possibilities and plans in Search and Explain. It also became obvious that the past is emotional and responses to the past need to be acknowledged in Uncover before people can move to the next question on the Frame. It became important to identify the significance and to allow the conversation to occur without interruption, for the process to be experienced in the present in Learn, before people could move to the next question. It was also evident once in Search and Explain, the future content and planning could be addressed. Using the conversation flow map it was easy for practitioners to see where people were in the process just by noticing who was talking to whom. Although the frame is presented as linear, the parties looped from the past through the present to the future and sometimes back and forth in a figure 8 until they had evidence that their responses had been acknowledged, their processes were complete and their content was understood. I saw these zones of past, present and future as another dimension of the frame and began to refer to them as Red for past, where things can stop without acknowledgement, Yellow for present, where caution and guidance may be required and Green for future, the signal for *go*, move on, advance to a better situation than the one you have been experiencing.

PULSE represents a pattern that can also be seen in other activities and process such as the writing, and research and planning processes that may be familiar to you. And so this book follows that pattern. In this *Prepare* chapter I have been doing most of the talking (writing) preparing you for the learning conversation that follows. I have identified process (PULSE) and protocol (GHOST), established "author"ity and confirmed the understanding that this is not meant to be a confidential conversation, established a five-chapter time frame. I have identified my role as author or conduit and yours as reader and contributor, now prepared with an explanation of the means of PULSE.

As the newest quote from my travel journal says "I have been a wanderer among distant fields. I have sailed down mighty rivers." To what Percy Bysshe Shelley has written I would add the words of another philosopher I know and admire who says "You know a dream is like a river, ever changing as it flows and the dream just a vessel that must follow where it goes ... so don't you sit upon the shoreline and say you're satisfied. Choose to chance the rapids and dare to dance the tides." Garth Brooks and I are on the river. Will you join us? Are you ready to proceed?

# Chapter 2: Uncover the Mystery

The front cover of this journal is an old map of the world. Where territory is uncharted there are pictures of dragons. "There be dragons" is what we say at PULSE when we are approaching uncharted territories in conversations as well. Each graduate from our PULSE Train the Trainer course receives a dragon and a ghost to remind them of the dangers and a way to overcome them. The ghost represents the gentle, honest, open, specific, talk protocol which plays an essential role in defining the PULSE appreciative approach. The dragon represents the mystery, the unknown and the possible danger inherent in any conversation.

This second chapter is written as a story of discovery, the *uncovering* of the frame as it occurred. It is about the past. It is emotional in the sense that it will evoke an emotional response in the telling and in the reading of it. It is different from the other chapters like Chapter 3, *Learn* where there is a present, active focus and Chapter 4, *Search* where there is a future, thought-provoking focus. Those of you in the heart triad of the Enneagram will enjoy this chapter and will relate to it more closely than to the other two. Just notice what has more appeal to you as a reader and use that information to learn a little about yourself.

It is mystery that we seek to uncover in the second piece of the PULSE conversation frame and in this second chapter of the book. PULSE is a process as you have heard it described in chapter one. It is also content and response. It is a way of feeling, acting and thinking about and in conversations. We know that the feeling or emotional aspect of conversation is rooted in the past circumstance. Your response to present situations relates to your own past experiences as you deconstruct and reconstruct your perceptions and therefore your reality.

This chapter sets out to outline the past circumstances of PULSE. Two stories will be presented. First you will read my story. It will outline the events or thoughts and sensations that lead me to pay more or less attention to one aspect or another of my own experience. The sum of those responses is described here as the Evolution of PULSE. Second is the other story, the events and publications of other people's thoughts on the subject of conversation. The purpose is to name the story.

## The Evolution of PULSE

As Confucius says at the top of *this* journal page "A journey of a thousand miles begins with a single step." The PULSE journey began when, as a teacher of gifted and talented students, I was challenged to learn more about thinking strategies and creative thinking so that I could more ably assist and challenge these young wizards. I realized that the journey that I began back then continues even today as I encounter again fellow travelers who have contributed to the thinking in the past and who now feel out of step with what has transpired since I last met them on the trail. PULSE is also traveling and evolving, a single step at a time. I have used the word evolution to describe the process of discovery because it has and continues to evolve.

Yesterday we sailed in San Diego. It was a glorious day with very little wind and I was reminded that a motor on a sailboat can be a good thing to have to keep you from going off course. So it is with friends and business associates who provide the energy to correct the course heading and point you once again toward your stated destination. The sailing metaphors abound in leader'ship'. There is a fleet of 'ships' such as ownership, stewardship, relationship, partnership, scholarship and others that lend their support to successful leadership. One year at the University of Lethbridge, my friend and co-teacher Carol Steen and I used the "ship" metaphor to talk about leadership with the students in the summer institute. It was interesting and fun. Because my dad had been a sailor in the Canadian Navy, I really enjoyed the experience. I felt safe with the language and with the concepts. Before the course was through we invited participants to write and think about their own metaphors for leadership. We talked about the power of the metaphor as a place to hook new learning to what we already know. As the story is told, as the mystery of PULSE is uncovered, the invitation to you the reader is to also think about your own story of uncovering the mystery of conversation. Look for the comparisons, the contrast, and the touch points, so that you will have something to hang this new perspective on and so that you and I can name this story together.

The evolution of PULSE began as I discovered with my grade 10 gifted students a process for creative thinking, a set of thinking strategies outlined in the 1980's by Joyce Juntune. Joyce had taken ideas from Edward De Bono and his six thinking hats and had created a binder full of thinking strategies for children in schools. The school division where I was working invited her to work with teachers in the division. I was chosen to or volunteered myself to represent my school on the committee that would supervise and champion the implementation. I was charged with learning the strategies and then presenting them to staff at monthly staff meetings. I also modeled the implementation in my own classroom and became very interested in how critical thinking and creative thinking were related. It was interesting to watch how the frame of the question could activate a different part of the brains and how a series of well framed questions could lead to a new and different outcome then what you might normally expect. I was hooked. As fate would have it an opportunity for me to move into administration at a smaller school which offered kindergarten to grade four presented itself about that time. If I accepted the position I would be both vice principal and teacher librarian. Until then I had always taught students who were physically bigger than me in junior and senior high schools but as the quote at the top of this travel journal page states "My favourite thing is to go where I have never gone." Diane Arbus and I shared that penchant for new adventures so I took the opportunity to change schools, grade levels, subject areas, roles and communities.

As teacher librarian I learned and taught about research. I helped students understand about research and how to use the library and as I was doing that I began to understand that the research process was a staged process just like the creative thinking process. At about the same time I was completing a final research paper for my Masters of Education degree and as I studied the writing processes I began to see the consistencies in all of the process: thinking, researching, writing and how they all linked and were in fact each part of a bigger pattern or process and how each could be broken down to other processes. As a teacher I was introduced to Madeline Hunter's approach to lesson planning and something called IOTA or Instrument for the Observation of Teaching Activities. As vice principal I was expected to evaluate teaching behaviour and again the pattern of the teaching process emerged as consistent with the other patterns and processes I had been studying.

As it happened I moved again from my position in elementary and primary schools to high school as a principal. It was there that I was first introduced to the ideas of William Glasser and his Choice Theory. Holding people and children capable became my way of interacting with the world after that. I also became very interested in mediation when I had the opportunity through a committee of the Alberta Teachers' Association to receive training with the Justice Institute of British Colombia. The instructor very skillfully 'manipulated' or structured the conversation to negotiate and mediate certain outcomes. I was introduced to the science of dialogue and through further research to mediation and Appreciative Inquiry. The importance of questions as guides reverberated for me. I hadn't considered conversation or any oral communication as needing structure the way that written communication such as research reports and lesson plans and thesis papers did. AH HA.

In my quest for more information I took training as a mediator and my friend Carol and I began to incorporate the mediation learning, theory and skills into the summer leadership institute programs at the University of Lethbridge. I came to understand that in fact the mediation skills were a core competency for leaders dealing with conflict on a daily basis. Working with the guidelines for speaking and listening in mediation we developed our own set, a protocol for listening and speaking to each other in a collaborative way. That is where the GHOST acronym was born. The strong link between the leadership and the mediation conversations and skills became apparent as did the power of the appreciative stance from Appreciative Inquiry and the holding people capable that came from William Glasser.

A new quote at the top of this journal page from "It's a wonderful Life" (1946) which is attributed to George Bailey says "I'm shaking the dust of this crummy little town off my feet and I'm going to see the world." That this quote should show up at the point in the story where I did just that is a little unnerving!! What happened next is that I gave up my principalship and moved to Calgary to work on my PhD, married a man who was born in 1946 (the year that "It's a Wonderful Life" was produced!) and have travelled the world. Since I made the move to Calgary I have studied leadership and conversation, learned to do mediation and to run a business.

While I was running the mediation business I made the acquaintance of Dan Dana who provided me with answers to questions about conversation that I had not found elsewhere in 240 hours of mediation training. "Why does dialogue work?" was my question. By the time I met Dan I had had enough experience as a mediator to know that it did work but it was his explanation of retaliatory and conciliatory cycles, Conflict Mountain and the concept of inhibitory reflex that gave me the scientific, physiological reason for what I had observed. Dan and I talked a lot about his perspectives and then one day Debra Dupree, who was Dan's chief operating officer at the time, called and I was invited to create a forty-hour mediation program to be offered all over the United States and Canada. I agreed. It was a swift journey from teacher, to mediator to mediation teacher. It was wonderful and exciting to teach the concepts and the skills because it gave me the opportunity to think more deeply about how mediation works and why.

In each training session I was asked questions. At one particular session I was challenged to clarify and defend my thinking around the deliberateness of each of the five stages in the new mediation model that I was using to train new mediators at the time. That model incorporated the work of Cheryl Picard and the thinking of Dan Dana around conflict resolution and holding people capable, as William Glasser had taught me to do, capable of resolving their own issues. The model was unique in the combination of the ideas and approaches of these authors and the language began to change and evolve as the distinctions between this new model and other models became clearer as a result of having to answer the hard questions posed by participants in the sessions around the US and Canada. Debra Dupree was a wonderful sounding board and critical friend as this evolution continued.

Paul Simon, one of my favourite poets just arrived at the top of this journal page. "I am more interested in what I discover than what I invent." What a perfect quote to describe the significance of what happened next. In my mediation business I met Steve Critchley, a soldier, retired from the Canadian Forces. Together we collaborated on a venture to put together an executive leadership training course that we called Beyond Leadership. It brought together his past military experience and the skills of conflict resolution as a core competency for leaders. He and I worked together to set up an outdoor adventure experience. We were planning for the program around the same time that I was writing my dissertation on leadership. I was analyzing data from interviews of leaders managing change and we were integrating the 16 steps of the Canadian Forces Battle Planning Procedures into the outline for the Beyond Leadership course. Steve was describing the steps and I was thinking about how there were too many for people to remember and that five was a good number, like the five steps in the mediation model we had been teaching. As he was talking I discovered that the five steps could be matched with the 16. He and I worked together to distill and define a five stage planning procedure for planning a task rather than a battle and for executing the plan. The first was *prepare* and it had sub-steps like warning orders. The second was *understand* the task. The third was *search, sort,* and *select* resources and processes; the fourth was *execute* and the fifth was *evaluate*. As we wrote them on the chart paper PULSE emerged. By then the PULSE Institute was four years old and had been in operation as a mediation and mediation training company teaching a five stage mediation process that looked like this:

1. Introduce the Process
2. Identify the Issues
3. Explore the Interests
4. Generate Options
5. Write an Agreement

The company had been named the PULSE Institute in 2002 when I had been working with a nurse on some training in hospitals for reducing conflict in surgical suites. Before that it was called Nancy Love Seminars. A friend had suggested the PULSE Institute as a name for a management consulting firm another friend of ours was starting up. The name resonated with me so I asked permission to use it and incorporated. Later, while teaching people to use language skills at the University of Lethbridge one summer, I sat up in bed in the middle of the night to the realization that PULSE stood for something ... People Using Language Skills Effectively. It became a mission statement and acrostic for PULSE all in one. *Now* I could see something else. A five stage *process*:

> Prepare for the process
>
> Uncover the Issue
>
> Learn the Interests
>
> Search the Options
>
> Explain the Memorandum of Understanding

This was close but was not quite consistent with the work I had been doing with the dissertation and sounded so much like the 'mediator speak' that participants in the workshops found challenging. Herman Melville is quoted here. "It is not down in any map; true places never are." PULSE is not down on any map. It remains the result of a journey of conversations with practitioners and the writing of a dissertation. The language of psychological deliberateness at each stage of the PULSE conversation eventually emerged and in the spring of 2005 the PULSE poster was born complete with conversation flow mapping and guiding questions on the side.

The PULSE checklist and script followed and we began to use the language from my dissertation:

Prepare for the Conversation

Uncover the Circumstances from the Past

Learn the Significance in the Present

Search the Possibilities of the Future

Explain in Writing a Plan of Action

## Transitions: Looping through the PULSE Zones

The key role for the leader of the conversations, it seemed to me, was to manage the transitions from one phase or zone to the other. The intent of each phase was clear and distinct and yet getting participants to move from one phase to the next was like pushing an amoeba across a street–difficult and tricky at times. As we used the frame, and the poster, we noticed that to move parties to the next frame it was helpful, even necessary, to write the answers to the guiding questions on chart paper and post them so that everyone could see. This moved the answers out into the light of day so to speak, naming elephants in a GHOSTly way, which seemed to move the parties from the past to the present and on to the future. At the end of each piece of the frame the PULSE practitioner would paraphrase, if appropriate and reframe the answers given into neutral or positive language and write the answers on the chart before moving to the next question. What I noticed was that they sometimes slipped back and forth between the Uncover and Learn, or went directly to Search. As the conversation lead, I had to listen carefully to hear where they were so that I could guide them to the next zone. Uncover the past was in the emotional Response Zone, what I began to call the Red Zone, and until the emotions were acknowledged the transition was not complete. Learn is where I saw parties moving through a change in perception, what I began to call the Process or Yellow Zone. Parties needed to be heard and a good paraphrase or reframe would normally allow them to move to the next zone. Search and Explain made up the Content or Green Zone where thinking was the key and parties were striving to be understood. Parties tended to circle in the Red Zone until some perception changed, usually because of new information on the table. The shift was often very evident. You could watch the physical change in people as they considered things differently, as the story changed for them. They would move through the Yellow Zone and into the Green Zone of conciliation where they could think and work together. It was like an infinity loop where parties would loop in the Red Zone for a while and then a conciliatory gesture was offered and they would bridge through the Yellow Zone to the Green Zone for a while and then something would trigger them to go back through the Red Zone for a loop or two and then back to the Green.

Left Circle

=

Red Zone

Right Circle

=

Green Zone

Centre Diamond = Yellow Zone

*Figure2: The PULSE Zones*

Although I had discovered a system or structure for conversations, and I knew that moving through the structure would get people to a resolution or a decision, I could see clearly that it was only a simple, linear structure on the face of it. In practice it requires flexibility as different personalities approached the conversation differently. The progression from the PULSE Red Zone through the Yellow to the Green requires skill and patience and understanding how and why different personality types approach the conversation. What I also noticed and became very curious about is how parties shift during the conversation and appear to emerge as 'different' people.

## Personalities in Conversation

Throughout this journey, another preoccupation of Carol's and mine was personality typing. We understood the value of valuing what you are not, especially for leaders, and each year as we planned our Summer Leadership Institute for the University of Lethbridge we would search out another way to type. What I saw in this new structure for conversations was a reflection of one of our personality typing tools, the Enneagram (see Figure 3). Adding to the discovery of the PULSE acronym in the frame, the coincidental mesh of the three personality types of the Enneagram which had become another passion of mine, felt like a leap in understanding for me. Each of the three categories of types has a preoccupation with the past, the present or the future. Heart types are preoccupied with the past. Body types are preoccupied with the present. Head types are preoccupied with the future. Even with a brief consideration of the Enneagram it became obvious to me why some people in mediated conversations became stuck at one or the other of the stages.

A closer examination revealed that heart types who live in the past need validation of their emotions before they can move on. Body types who live in the present need to understand the present situation before they can move on. Head types like to move directly to the future and plan for the next event. It became clear that in order to meet the needs of all of the types, a structure that allotted time and consideration to each of the time zones, past, present and future would lead to more effective communication for everyone.

The leaders in my PhD study had taught me that to be effective, each conversation needed to include a consideration of the past, the present and the future. The processes and the patterns from Joyce Juntune in the 1980's through to Love 2006 were consistent and descriptive of how effective communication occurs. Once a person realizes that conversations go through the time zones, they can use the structure to ensure effective communication and it becomes their secret weapon, a secret weapon that can be used to slay dragons.

## The Other Story

Throughout the last three decades other writers have ventured into the study of conversation. That preoccupation can be seen in book titles like *Fierce Conversations, Crucial Conversations, Difficult Conversations* and *Discussing the Undiscussables*. Although the authors have all made a case for a certain type of conversation, little time or energy is devoted to the *how* of these conversations. Authors agree that conversation is important and that they are necessary, especially the difficult ones. What is missing in the literature is a description of the techniques and structure and skills that will successfully guide a conversation through the zones from beginning to satisfying end.

Meanwhile advances in the study of Appreciative Inquiry have been made and it is becoming more and more mainstream to think about issues and concerns from a positive or appreciative perspective. Authors like Whitney and Trosten-Bloom, Cooperrider and others have been advancing the thinking and raising the awareness of the practice of Appreciative Inquiry through the World Wide Web and publication of books and research to support the arguments for an appreciative stance. My own research which took the form of an Appreciative Portraiture, relied heavily on the principles of Appreciative Inquiry.

Another indication of advanced thinking in this area is the plethora of books on the Enneagram that are becoming popular. A Google search reveals hundreds of sites and book titles on the subject. Enough people have come in contact with the Enneagram so that it has reached its *tipping point*: that point where it becomes a household word, where people sharing their experiences with it are finding others with similar experiences and word is spreading fast.

Given the expanding knowledge and literature on the topics of conversation, the Enneagram, leadership, Appreciative Inquiry and more, the shared title of the story becomes Conversations for Change. The connection between my study of mediation and my study of leaders is that it all happens in conversation.

Understanding the nuances and the skills of conversation improves them and by improving conversations we can improve relationships.  This book is about all conversations that lead to a change in relationship, in organizational structure, in the way we do things around here.  It is about a dragon slayer named PULSE, a frame for conversations that incorporates the latest thinking in its deliberate approach to conversations, relationships and organizations that matter.

# Chapter 3: Learn the Meaning

It is the significance of the discovery of a simple frame for conversations that inspires awe in me. Conversations are the life blood of organizations and of relationships. PULSE provides evidence that information is flowing through the organization to rejuvinate it and keep it healthy. What is an organization without conversations? It is difficult to determine. Is there an organization without conversation? The evolution of the system into the PULSE frame, the consistency of it, allows people to take control, to get in shape and to maintain healthy relationships.

Learn in the PULSE frame asks the question, "Why is this important?" This chapter answers that question about the frame. There are three main reasons that the PULSE frame is important. PULSE contributes to an understanding of the relationship response area, the PULSE Red Zone, by integrating the use of the Enneagram as a means of understanding what pasts and motivations people bring to conversations and how they change as they move through the process. PULSE also contributes to understanding the process of conversations, where and how perceptions are changed in the present, in the PULSE Yellow Zone, by integrating the work of Dan Dana and his explanation of the theory of conciliation. PULSE contributes to the understanding of the concepts and content aspects of conversation as well with its acceptance of the appreciative stance that invites people to a positive future in the PULSE Green Zone.

Examining each, content, process and response, will provide suggestions to describe ways in which PULSE is significant. By integrating the thinking from different sources, PULSE adds meaning to existing understanding of structures in conversation that already exist in the literature and in practice. In approaching the explanation in this way, what will also become clear are the criteria that define a PULSE conversation and a PULSE practitioner.

## Learn 1

## Enneagram: A Significant Response

At PULSE we talk about criteria a lot. For us it is the piece that is missing from other types of conversations. Identifying the criteria for a better future before creating a plan gives the plan a solid base and ensures that everyone's needs are met. We require PULSE practitioners to develop an understanding of the Enneagram.

Enneagram means nine points on a circle in Greek. I discovered the Enneagram ten or fifteen years ago when I was teaching with Carol Steen at the University of Lethbridge. We needed another perspective on personality typing. We had used the True Colours, which was based on the Myers Briggs Type Indicator. We had used the Thomas Kilmann instrument. We had used the Personality Compass and others. I was clear that not one of these typing systems provided the whole picture. Each revealed a little more about "self" and was helpful in that it provided another view or filter on how to categorize the world or people. Using only one system in a course led to stereotyping rather than to the use of typing as a tool. For me it was important to give people a lens or lenses through which to expand their perspective of the people in the world, not to narrow their vision. As often as we encouraged that expansion, each typing exercise served to narrow the dialogue of types and categories at least over the short term of the course.

In my search for new ways and strategies for leaders to deal with and understand themselves and others, I stumbled upon the Enneagram, an ancient yet modern way of identifying what motivates people. There was a quality about this symbol and what it represented that acknowledged why people behave in different ways in different situations. The Enneagram also identified valid and valued travel paths for when situations change. The fluid, dynamic nature of the diagram and the types made sense to me. The Enneagram is simple yet complex, just like the PULSE frame and the people I deal with every day.

"The only way to catch a train I have ever discovered is to miss the one before." A quote from G K Chesterton that was true for me in this situation. During the first encounter I had had with the Enneagram at the University of Lethbridge, although I had seen its relevance and application to leadership, I had missed the 'train' on how it contributed to conversation. Once I stepped onto this train of thought I could see the view from the inside, the journey that it takes people on is fascinating, enlightening and useful. The Enneagram is simple yet complex. There is beauty in its simplicity and strength in its complexity, and it is one of the constructs that adds strength to the PULSE frame.

## Enneagram Triads

The Enneagram identifies nine types, three in each of three triads. Beginning with the triads it is easy to find evidence of the Enneagram's truth in everyday language. The three triads or centers as they are sometimes called are Body, Head and Heart and for me, they identify the three kinds of people I know in the world. Body people live in the present and in their bodies. They are always moving, doing, and taking action. Their language reflects their preoccupation with the present and with "doing". If something happens to you, they ask "What are you doing about it?" Head people live in the future and in their thoughts. They are always thinking and their preoccupation with the future is reflected in their language. They plan, scheme, dream and think and so when something happens to you they ask "What's your plan?" or "What will you do next?" Heart people live in the past and in their hearts. They emote, feel, and experience things at the emotional level. They are preoccupied with feelings and it is reflected in their language. When something happens to you they say "How did that make you feel?" The nine types are assigned numbers. Their descriptions follow. Their positions on the diagram and within the types is illustrated below.

The triads are referred to as The Instinctive Triad (Body), The Thinking Triad (Head) and The Feeling Triad (Heart) and each includes three numbered types. Each triad includes an introvert, an extrovert and a centred personality type. People emerge from childhood with one of the nine types dominating their personality, with a basic enneatype. The type reveals what motivates them and takes into account the nature and the nurture aspects of our development as human beings. The types are numbered and no one is better or worse than the other. They indicate instead, a different perspective or world view. What is interesting is that once you have determined your basic type you will also recognize the direction you travel in stress and in growth and how an adjacent number serves as your wing. Each type also has nine levels of development that move from unhealthy or destructive to healthy and liberating. On the surface, a quick study of the Enneagram provides a fuzzy view of how people respond in conversation. With further study into this complex, vital work, the picture becomes clearer.

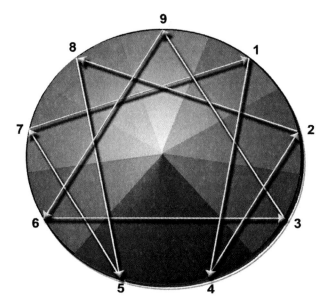

*Figure 3: The Enneagram: Body(8, 9, 1), Head(5, 6, 7), Heart(2, 3, 4), showing stress lines.*

Helen Keller is quoted here in my journal. She reminds us that "Life is either daring adventure or nothing." Adventure is a wonderful word that can mean different things to different people. For each of the nine types, because of their differing motivations and world views, the word adventure would conjure up different thoughts, feelings and actions. Defining what an adventure is for each of the nine Enneagram types will provide some insight into how each of the nine types experiences the world and what motivates them. I have identified first the number and then their respective triads in the descriptions that follow. A chart that indicates the travel paths of each type as they move from the PULSE Red Zone, Yellow Zone and Green Zone follows the descriptions and provides additional information on how the knowledge of the Enneagram assists PULSE practitioners in their work.

***Ones: Active Present.*** Ones get their energy from order. They are the introverts in the body triad. An adventure for a one would be well organized and would meet a preordained set of standards. Ones live in the present and strive for perfection which is both their vice and their virtue. A one is motivated by standardization and organization. They seek to avoid mistakes and can be viewed as rigid and unbending. Ones are the people in your office with neat desks and organized minds who also want to straighten you and your environment. They follow the rules and seek to set and meet standards.

When ones are stressed they move toward a four. On the positive side they become artistic and on the negative side they become depressive. Relaxed ones go to seven where, on the positive side they see possibilities and become light hearted, or, on the negative side they back out of responsibilities. If a one is in conflict, what might be missing for them would include order, personal control, standardization, routine, predictability, approval, and justice. Ones expect people, including themselves, to be on their best behaviour.  They are principled, self controlled, purposeful and perfectionistic.

**Twos: Emotional Past.** Twos, who are the extraverts of the Heart triad, get their energy from helping others and from generally being helpful.  They are motivated by their contributions to other people and may sometimes neglect their own needs or become vengeful when favours or considerations are not reciprocated.  They live in the past and in emotion and yet rarely share their own feelings except to manipulate others into doing what they feel is best for the other person.  They seek appreciation and situations where they feel needed.  They avoid feeling unworthy and an adventure for them would be one where they could be the Sherpa.

Twos who are stressed move to eight.  On the positive side they can be clearer about what they want for themselves but on the negative side they can become impulsive and angry or want to take control of things by force.  When twos are relaxed they move to four. On the positive side they pay more attention to their own feelings and develop an aesthetic appreciation. On the negative side they can be consumed by melancholy.  When twos are in conflict, what might be missing for them would include recognition, appreciation, opportunities to contribute, inclusion, approval, dependability and some return of affection. Twos give and they care.  They are demonstrative, generous, people pleasing and possessive.

**Threes: Emotional Past.** For threes an adventure would involve achievement and accomplishments combined with recognition and attention.  Threes also live in emotion and in the past but they are more about themselves then twos.  Threes are the centre of the Heart Triad and can appear at times to be emotionless when they are overcome with emotion. They are motivated by success. They are sometimes referred to as the performer because they are motivated by being in the limelight and being centre stage. Threes seek respect and admiration and avoid failure.

When threes are stressed they move to nine. On the positive side they see things from different perspectives and take interest in others. On the negative side they become indecisive and evasive. When they are relaxed they move to six where on the positive side they develop loyalties and on the negative side they become fearful and suspicious. Threes like to achieve and lead. They are adaptive, driven, image conscious and they excel at whatever they do.

**Fours: Emotional Past.** An adventure for a four would have to be something that no one else had ever done in quite the same way. Fours are motivated by being different and unique. They are the introverted side of the Heart Triad and get their energy from demonstrating core values and by separating themselves from the crowd. Drama is a word that you might associate with fours. Everything they do is bigger and better and definitely different. Uniforms are not for fours. They seek to express deep feelings and connections unique to them and they avoid rejection.

When a four is stressed they move to two. On the positive side, they become generous and giving. On the negative side, they become possessive and demanding. When fours are relaxed they move to one. On the positive side, they like to get things right and in order.  On the negative side, they obsess.  If a four is in conflict what might be missing for them would include autonomy, uniqueness, an opportunity to be creative, one-on-one connection time, beauty, aesthetic, empathy and profound communication.  For fours it is important to be true to themselves.  They are expressive, dramatic, self absorbed and temperamental.

**Fives: Thoughtful Future.**  An adventure for a five could take place without leaving the room.  Reading a good book or considering a new way of looking at something, a new idea or concept, in an uninterrupted environment, can be very adventurous for a five.  If they do travel, they are happy to do it alone.  Fives are analytical.  They get their energy from watching observing, thinking.  They value detachment and spending time alone.  Fives can be impatient with those they deem to be less intelligent or capable then they are.  Fives are the introvert of the Head Triad and they live in a world of concepts, thinking and planning the future, developing theories.  They seek knowledge and wisdom and they avoid intrusion.

Fives under stress move to seven.  On the positive side, they become fun loving adventurers.  On the negative side, they abandon responsibility.  A relaxed five moves toward eight.  On the positive side, they take up the cause and take charge.  On the negative side, they become confrontational and bossy.  If they are in conflict what might be missing for them would include autonomy, information, data, competence, analysis, time to think things through.  Fives are perceptive, innovative, mysterious, secretive and isolated.

**Sixes: Thoughtful Future.**  For sixes an adventure would be to visit a familiar and safe place with loyal friends. They would be skeptical and uncertain with unfamiliarity. Sixes are motivated by a sense of security and safety. They represent the centre of the Head Triad and can 'think too much' about the future and become worried and suspicious of what MIGHT happen. Sixes are loyal. They seek meaning and certainty and trust. They avoid negativity and threats.

A six under stress moves to a three. On the positive side, they become ambitious and achieve wonderful things. On the negative side, they become arrogant and driven. A relaxed six moves toward nine. On the positive side, they become agreeable and accommodating. On the negative side, they become couch potatoes. If a six is in conflict, what might be missing would include safety, loyalty, team work, confidence, reliability. Sixes believe that you should stick with what you know. They are engaging, responsible, anxious and suspicious.

***Sevens: Thoughtful Future.*** Sevens are adventurers, optimistic scenario builders. An adventure for a seven would be a dizzying array of new and exciting things to do and think about. They are the multi-taskers. They live in their heads and in the future and are always looking for the next event or gig or project. Sevens have strong openings and weak closings. Getting a seven to complete a project, when a new one is waiting for their attention, can be difficult. They are the extraverts of the Head types. They seek stimulation and pleasure. They avoid boredom and discomfort.

Stressed sevens move to one. On the positive side, they bring order out of the chaos of their world. On the negative side, they become obsessive compulsive. Relaxed, a seven will move toward five. On the positive side, they become thoughtful, pensive and insightful.   On the negative side, they become reclusive.   If a seven is in conflict what might be missing for them would include creativity, stimulation, variety, opportunity, hopefulness, optimism, flexibility or the option to escape.   Sevens believe in staying positive come what may. They are spontaneous, versatile, distractible and scattered.

**Eights: Active Present.** For an eight, an adventure would have a just cause and would have them in charge.  Eights are motivated by being in control of the situation and by justice.  They are the extraverts of the Body Triad.  When they are angry people know.  They are the perfect people to have in case of emergency or where a project needs to get done.  They are doers and can move things forward, sometime with little regard for others.  They are practical and direct, what you see is what you get.

An eight under stress moves toward five.  On the positive side, they become perceptive and thoughtful. On the negative side, they become isolated and uncommunicative.  Relaxed eights move toward two. On the positive side, they become demonstrative and generous.   On the negative side, they become possessive and vindictive.  If eights are in conflict what might be missing for them would include fairness, justice, directness, action, power, leadership, control and competence, a task well done.  Eights believe in testing people out to see what they are made of.  They are self-confident, decisive, willful and confrontational.

**Nines: Active Present.** For nines an adventure could very well happen on their couch in their living room. Although they are in the Body Triad, nines often "don't move much" out of fear of unbalancing things. They are the centre of the Body Triad.  Nines believe in a simple, easy going approach to life.  They seek harmony and want everyone to get along. They avoid conflict. They are the peacemakers.

Stressed nines move to six. On the positive side, they become engaging and loyal. On the negative side, they become suspicious of everything and everyone. Relaxed nines move to three. On the positive side, they become ambitious and adaptive and get things done. On the negative side, they become driven and obsessed with success. If they are in conflict what might be missing for them would include harmony, compatibility, simplicity, dignity, inclusiveness, flexibility. Keeping it simple and peaceful keeps nines happy. They are receptive, reassuring, agreeable to a fault and complacent.

| PULSE Red Zone stressed | PULSE Yellow Zone Basic Enneatypes striving for …. | PULSE Green Zone relaxed |
|---|---|---|
| 4 | 1– perfection | 7 |
| 8 | 2– connection | 4 |
| 9 | 3– success | 6 |
| 2 | 4– differentiation | 1 |
| 7 | 5– detachement | 8 |
| 3 | 6– security | 9 |
| 1 | 7– excitement | 5 |
| 5 | 8– power | 2 |
| 6 | 9– peace | 3 |

Enneagram Travel Paths

The Enneagram provides a tool for identifying what is missing for people, what their criteria for resolution or decision are. In conversation, knowing the Enneagram types assists the delta or practitioner to know what to acknowledge for parties to feel that they can move past any disagreements to resolution. Understanding that there are nine types, in three categories or triads, one focused on the past and emotions, one preoccupied with the present and doing and the third planning a future, thinking and conceptualizing, explains why people behave the way they do in the conversation. Unlike other personality typing, the Enneagram considers the motivation behind the behaviour rather than the behaviour itself and recognizes the travel paths that parties take as they move from the Red Zone, through Yellow to Green. It also takes into account the influence of the number next to your basic Enneatype which is referred to as a wing or a shadow. The wing refers to the strong characteristics of the adjacent type whereas the shadow refers to its darker side. Each of us can identify a dominate wing, one of the adjacent numbers that influences more than the other.

**Head: Thoughtful Futures.** Five, six and seven types make up the Head Triad. These types are preoccupied with the future. The language that they use relates to thinking and planning. When they come into a conversation they have usually thought of a solution already and are eager to forget the past and move on. For practitioners of PULSE, knowing that people will come prepared to resolve is important. For these people it is necessary to slow things down and have them consider new information that may cause them to think differently about the situation.

**Heart: Emotional Pasts.** Twos, threes and fours make up the Heart Triad. These people are preoccupied with the past. Their language is usually past tense and focused on emotion. Knowing that people come to conversations needing to have their emotions acknowledged is good information for practitioners. Members of the Heart Triad will hold on to their version of the past until the emotions are acknowledged. Only then will it be possible for them to consider a different version of the story.

**Body: Active Present.** Ones, eights and nines make up the Body Triad. People who identify themselves as body types are active. Their language is full of action words and is present focused. Knowing that these types are motivated by what is happening in the present equips the practitioner to move them back to the past and then through the present to the future in a deliberate manner. This allows Body types to experience the situation differently.

## PULSE Triads

Knowing the Enneagram allows you to value all of these types and the contributions they can make to resolution and decision. In Prepare, people from each triad show up differently. People from the Head Triad will show an immediate concern for content; people from the Heart Triad will be demonstratively emotional in their response; and people from the Body Triad will be present and engaged with the process. In Uncover heart types of the emotional past dominate until acknowledged, the body types of the active present want to get on with it, while the head types of the thoughtful future already have things solved. In Learn, the active present dominates. In Search and Explain the thoughtful future is more engaged. Integrating the use of the Enneagram into the PULSE frame contributes to the study of conversation by adding knowledge and understanding to the relational response of pratitioners. Knowing and expecting the triads to be motivated in a certain way and by certain beliefs, expectations, assumptions, concerns and hopes prepares a PULSE practitioner to be more effective and allows them to create a greater sense of satisfaction with the process for everyone. The artful balance of content, process and response in the PULSE Conversation is the PULSE CPR.

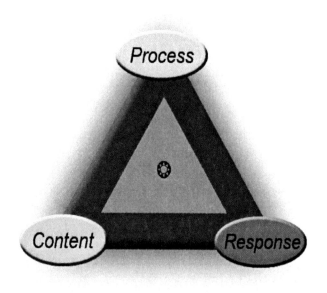

*Figure 4: The PULSE CPR*

\* \* \*

A quote from Henry Miller just appeared at the top of this journal page. "One's destination is never a place, but rather a new way of looking at things." The Enneagram offers a new way of looking at things, a new lens through which people can view the world and the people in it. The Enneagram is not *the* answer. It is *an* answer to the question of how we understand what motivates people in conversation. One of its most compelling attributes is that it is not static. The Enneagram wings and the stress and security lines give evidence of the dynamic nature of people and how they respond and react differently in different situations. They act or react like a different person because their motivations change. It is the acceptance of people as complex, maturing beings that attracts me to the Enneagram. I invite you to learn more.

The dragon or caution in the use of the Enneagram, as with any personality typing system, is that if you are looking for a certain behaviour or attribute then that is what you see.Chris Argyris and his Ladder of Inference explains that people observe the same data, choose from that data what to pay attention to, add their own meaning, make assumptions, draw conclusions, adopt beliefs and take action in the blink of an eye. With the *reflexive loop* Argyris explains how we select data based on the belief and assumptions that we made in the first instance, perpetuating the distortion of information. You see what you are looking for and you hear what you are expecting to hear. Knowing this allows you to think, feel and experience more deeply and be more deliberate about hearing and seeing a wider range of motivation.

In our workshops we use marbles to represent the Enneagram. Marbles, like people, are each a unique combination of the same elements. How you look at it, your perspective, and what you are looking for determines what you see in a marble and in a person. The Enneagram lets you value what you are not and helps you understand what motivates people to behave in the ways that they do in conflict. It is a wonderful tool to rely on when moving from Uncover to Learn and from Learn to Search. It is another layer of the PULSE frame that adds to its complexity and gives it strength.

## Learn 2

## Managing Differences: Significant Process

From a social, emotional or behavioural point of view, the PULSE frame relies on the Enneagram to understand the motivation for the way that people behave in conversation, by understanding how they approach the world. The Enneagram provides the filter for understanding what people bring from the past to the PULSE conversation. In the present, in the moment of conversation, what happens is best understood by examining the work of Dan Dana. Physiologically the PULSE frame relies on his explanation of what happens in conversation.

In the 1980's Dana identified four forces toward harmony at work in conversation. His work described conflictual or difficult conversations. He defines conflict as any situation where anger is present and talks about the cycles of conflict. Dana described the retaliatory cycle. In the retaliatory cycle, one person does something that becomes a trigger. The other person perceives a threat, becomes angry and then behaves in one of two ways. Either they walk away or they power play. These choices represent the fight or flight instincts that humans have used to survive. Either of these choices can be perceived as a threat by the other party and the cycle continues and puts the relationship in jeopardy. The third choice is dialogue which is often counterintuitive but can be very successful. In dialogue the forces toward harmony work their magic.

Dana stated that a 90 minute conversation is enough time for the forces to work and allow parties to switch from the retaliatory cycle to the conciliatory cycle. In conciliation, one party makes a conciliatory gesture, what Dana identifies as an expression of *voluntary vulnerability* (2005, p.150-166). The other party has what he called an *inhibitory reflex*, the inhibition of aggression that occurs in social animals when one submits to the other. Dana suggests that the inhibitory reflex is 'hard wired' into human beings like fight or flight. What happens in dialogue is that one party expresses an apology or a both-gain approach or self discloses and the other accepts the gesture and reciprocates with a conciliatory gesture of their own. The conciliatory cycle continues and moves the parties closer together building the relationship. Evidence of both cycles can be found in dialogue. In a 90 minute dialogue the forces toward harmony work to change the cycles.

## The Four Forces of Harmony
*Fatigue* is the first of the four forces toward harmony. People get tired of fighting or avoiding because it takes energy to perpetuate a dispute. Fatigue alone will not necessarily lead to resolution although some people do give up or give in when exhaustion hits. *A desire for*

*peace* is the second force. We all have, as human beings, an inborn desire for peace. It can be operationalized differently. Some people make war to create peace. The motive is always peace or the world as 'I' would have it, keeping in mind that there would be nine ways to define a peaceful world as understood through the Enneagram. In fact as humans we cannot disagree with ourselves because that causes dissonance and could lead to psychosis.

The third force is *catharsis,* that sense of relief you get once you've said your piece, unloaded or said what you've been thinking and the sky doesn't fall. Many people hold on to valuable information, afraid of the consequences of sharing. Once they have shared the 'secret', they experience a sense of relief. The PULSE frame and protocol encourages full disclosure for the reason that if information is withheld in a conversation, it becomes obvious: there is an elephant in the room and it may become necessary to go elephant hunting as the PULSE practitioner. If people leave the conversation with more to say, the quality of the resolution is compromised. That is why the PULSE frame invites parties to say what they're thinking, to be honest and to be open to hearing the other person's story and allowing it to influence them. Parties will feel comfortable to disclose at different points in the conversation. When they do, catharsis will be evident physiologically. The change in state represents an adaptation to acceptance as parties move from retaliation to conciliation.

T. S. Elliot wrote "Only those who will risk going too far can possibly find out how far one can go". Creating an environment for conversation where parties feel that they can say what they're thinking, where they can risk vulnerability, is the task of the PULSE practitioner.

Expressions of voluntary vulnerability and a response which Dan Dana calls the *inhibitory reflex* provides the fourth force towards harmony. Dana explains that people move from retaliation, or what he calls the wrong reflexes of fight or flight, to conciliation through the inhibitory reflex where they also demonstrate voluntary vulnerability with a reciprocal conciliatory gesture. The way I have experienced it through PULSE is that if an action is perceived as a threat, the response is anger and the reflex is fight, flight or freeze. In the amygdale or reptilian brain, decisions are made about the action that is taken next. If an action is perceived as a conciliatory gesture then the response is a sense of connection, a collective consciousness experience and the reflex is to release the aggression, relax and relate to the other party.

The path is like a figure eight, as described in Figure 2: sometimes staying in retaliation for a long time and then moving with one perception change to conciliation. Other times the change in perception is quicker and the parties move quickly into conciliation based on one new piece of information. Generally it takes reframing of the circumstance or the significance of the event to move from one zone to the other. The PULSE Red Zone is consistent with Dana's cycle of retaliation and is about the emotional past. If the emotions are acknowledged and parties feel heard they can move from the Red Zone to the Yellow Zone where perceptions change.

The appreciative stance of the PULSE frame and the skilled PULSE practitioner can shed new light and allow for a change in perception with the use of the PULSE skills for reframe. PULSE practitioners look for what is working for the parties and will focus attention on the positive aspects of the situation. Parties can then move to the Green Zone of conciliation where there is a future focus. The Green Zone is where calmer heads prevail. PULSE practitioners focus on moving people from where they are through the past, to the present, and then to the future. The PULSE frame is constructed so that the conversation will pass through each of the zones. Dana's Retaliatory Cycle explained the Red Zone phenomenon that I had seen. His Conciliatory Cycle explained the Green Zone in the PULSE frame and his Forces Toward Harmony explain what had to happen in the Yellow Zone, the dialogue, for parties to bridge from one zone to the other.

Clifton Fadiman's quote from the top of this page reads, "When you travel, remember that a foreign country is not designed to make you comfortable. It is designed to make its own people comfortable." Such is the journey through the time zones and the PULSE frame. The positive questions and the appreciative stance, the future and solution focus all seem counterintuitive at times. "This is not how people talk" I hear from participants and it is true. Often people talk *at* each other rather than *with* each other. Often people don't spend enough time in conversation to allow the forces towards harmony to work.

## Climbing Conflict Mountain
Dana identified 90 minutes as the amount of time necessary to guarantee that retaliation will turn to conciliation. He described Conflict Mountain as a jagged confrontational front slope with a smoother, shorter conciliatory slope on the down side and a breakthrough at the peak. The jagged front slope shows the forays into the conciliatory zone that can lead back to retaliation from time to time. His contention is that if people agree not to walk away (flee) or power play (fight), if they agree to stay with

the process for 90 minutes, the forces will work and parties will begin to recognize the conciliatory gestures as conciliation and connection and not threat. Many conversations don't last 90 minutes. In those kinds of conversations parties remain on the confrontation side of the mountain not allowing themselves to reach the peak the breakthrough that moves them to the Green Zone of conciliation. The conflict mountain described by Dana and the Ladder of Inference described by Argryis both rely on climbing up and down to get to resolution. Argryis's reflexive loop shows how parties get stuck in their own version of things and changing perception can be difficult. I saw Dana's mountain climbing equipment (supporting concilitory gestures) as a way to take people back down the Ladder to the breakthrough and to conciliation.

So when participants tell me that "People don't talk this way" I say "People who are still in conflict don't. People who have come to resolution and decisions do." PULSE is a discovery. It represents what happens when conversations are successful. My own research indicates that time zone sensitive conversations are the key to managing change. Other frames and structures for conversations have elements of the frame. Sales conversations for example, contain the elements of prepare for the conversation, uncover what the customer is looking for, learn their criteria, search possibilities and explain the deal. So, in fact, people do talk this way.

It is this PULSE kind of conversation that can successfully take people back down the Ladder of Inference, a ladder they climb up without a nanosecond of consideration. Malcolm Gladwell talks about these same phenomena in *Blink*. He talks about a Theory of Thin Slices where decisions are often made on very little information. These instantaneous decisions can be just as well informed if the people making them are experts in their field. People will quickly see or hear what they are looking for or what they expect to see or hear in a given situation. If they are looking for something positive, that is what they will find. If they are expecting something negative, again, that is what they will notice. This is also referred to as the *self-fulfilling prophecy* and has been documented in research in many fields. In the PULSE conversation the focus of what people have experienced in the past is changed so that they can consider a new story with a different past, present and future. The power of reframe exposes the existing perspective and invites people to consider a different, more positive one.

Asking people to take a new stance so that they can change their perspective can be interesting and is what PULSE practitioners do in a PULSE conversation. Whether people are on the Ladder of Inference or on Conflict Mountain they take a stance or perspective that looks back to the past or forward to the future. The perspective or *perch* of the viewer can influence what is seen or heard in a conversation as well and that is why the *stance* or *perch* or *perspective* of the delta, the PULSE practitioner, is so important. That leads me to the next significant factor influencing the PULSE frame ... The Appreciative Stance.

### The Appreciative Stance: Significant Content

In the 1980s, David Cooperrider noticed that if you ask people about negative situations you learn more and get more information about negativity and create more negative situations. If you change the question and ask what's good about a situation, the result is that you hear stories about the positive aspects and can improve morale and you can change perspectives people have of the past, the present and the future. Telling the good story allows people to experience the situation differently. His work evolved into a body of literature called Appreciative Inquiry. It is appreciative in that it shows appreciation or gratitude or respect and it adds value. It is inquiry because the question is the thing: the framing of the question is the pivotal point for how people respond to situations.

**The Constructivist Principle.** Underlying assumptions accepted by Appreciative Inquiry included the Constructivist Principle which states that we create ourselves and our experiences. We are "linguistically constructed relational selves" as Cooperrider states. Our language informs and then forms our thoughts, actions and responses. "Words create worlds." Evidence of this principle in action abound. Our basic understanding of the Enneagram begins with peoples' choice of vocabulary which provides evidence of their motivation from past, present, to future.

"I never traveled without my diary. One should always have something sensational to read in the train." Oscar Wilde was constructing his own reality, his own version of the truth of his life in his diary. Similarly, you and I can change a situation or our experience of it by changing the words we use to think about the situation. It is this ability to create a new perspective through an appreciative, positive lens that adds strength and complexity to the PULSE frame. Reframing the past, the present, and the future by asking different questions from a positive, appreciative stance is the key. Choosing words in a deliberate way, ones that emphasize the positive, the solution and the future, rather than dwelling in the past and in the problem. Moving people from the past may require a reframe of the story. Moving people from the present situation requires an identification of the criteria for resolution or solution. Moving people to the future, a positive future, full of possibilities, is the main focus of the PULSE Frame and choosing in a way in a very deliberate way, the words used to describe the past, present, and future of the situation accomplishes that. Words create worlds. Words change perception and allow parties to move from retaliation, or the Red Zone of the past emotionality, through the Yellow Zone where perceptions are changed by identifying criteria to the Green Zone of conciliation or future-focused solutions and ideas. We live in a world of perceptions. Using words to change these perceptions is where the strength of the PULSE frame can be found.

***The Poetic Principle.*** Another underlying principle of Appreciative Inquiry is the Poetic Principle. It suggests that pasts, presents and futures are endless sources of information. Think of the infinite interpretations of any line of poetry. The Poetic Principle requires you to look at things honestly from an appreciative stance looking for what is good, what you want more of, rather than what is not good. Our definition of good and not good are socially conditioned and will vary. The Enneagram, with its information about what motivates people, helps us to understand why the definitions of good and the criteria for resolution differ. Focusing on a positive interpretation, a reframe from an appreciative perspective can change the perceptions and the outcome of any conversation.

***The Simultaneity Principle.*** Change begins the moment we ask a question. This is the Simultaneity Principle. As soon as the question is asked, people begin to think differently about a situation. You commonly hear "I've never thought about that" and that is why that type of question is critical. In the PULSE frame the questions are framed to lead to resolution. "What are you here to resolve or decide today?" That question is deliberately worded to focus on the future, on solution. If you were to ask "What brought you here?" or "What seems to be the problem?" then you'll hear about the emotionality from the past. "What are you to resolve today?" allows a participant to identify the circumstance without dwelling on all the hurt and anxiety that may have resulted.

**The Anticipatory Principle.** Walt Whitman has just arrived on this journey with a quote that explains, in an elegant way, situations or as he calls them 'lands' and how we become part of that landscape whatever it is, or whatever we perceive it to be. He says "O lands! O all so dear to me-what you are, I become part of that, whatever it is". If as PULSE practitioners we ask questions that allow people to dwell in negative landscapes then they will. If in fact we can ask questions that adjust the perspective to a more positive frame, then people will also move toward appreciation. It is the heliotropic principle at work. People, like plants, move toward what nourishes and nurtures. What we pay attention to, is what we get more of in conversation so it becomes important in the PULSE frame to stay focused on the positive and to ask questions that allow conversation participants to do the same.

In Learn we ask, for example, "What's important to you about your circumstance?" instead of "What was the impact?" The impact question takes people back to the emotionality of the past. The "What's important?" question invites them to identify their underlying

Beliefs, Expectations, Assumptions, Concerns, and Hopes, (the BEACH) to identify what has been missing for them in this situation which forms the criteria that will be satisfied in order for the resolution or solution to be sustainable.

In Search, we ask "What could you do to resolve the circumstance and meet your criteria?" it is deliberately focused on future possibilities, options for resolution, and in the Explain frame we ask "What would you like your plan to say?" In all frames and especially in these last two, the questions are deliberately chosen to reflect that the parties in the conversation own the outcome. My friend Carol says "You don't take care of what you don't own". At any time in the conversation, if other people's thoughts and ideas are included, then the sustainability of the outcome is jeopardized. So the questions are worded to reflect ownership of the outcome, the plan, the image of the future of the parties, the one they create together. Positive images create positive futures. That is the Anticipatory Principle of the Appreciative Inquiry method. Argyris' Ladder of Inference and reflexive loop supports this concept. In fact we see what we are looking for; we hear what we are listening for; and if we create or imagine or anticipate a positive future we will find one. The PULSE frame demonstrates a clear understanding of the Anticipatory Principle. From the beginning of the PULSE conversation, parties anticipate a mutually agreeable plan of action. They anticipate that the conversations will be gentle and honest and open and that they will be expected to be specific and to talk: to say what they are thinking. They anticipate that they will be answering questions, positive questions, and moving toward a future that is different from the past that brought them there. In anticipating these things, the conversation lead or delta co-creates the GHOST protocol and the balanced outcome with the participants. It is a very subtle acceptance of the principles, constructivist, poetic, simultaneity and anticipatory, that gives the PULSE frame the strength and accounts for its continued success.

**The Positive Principle.** Combine this knowledge with the acceptance of the Positive Principle, which simply stated is that it feels good to feel good, and you begin to see how the PULSE frame creates a situation where positive emotions can broaden the scope of possibilities, present and future actions, and plans. Positive emotions can undo negative ones and build resiliency and can move people from the past, from the Red Zone, through changing perceptions in the Yellow Zone, to a positive future and the Green Zone. Focusing on the positive core, the underlying beliefs, expectations, assumptions, concerns and hopes (the BEACH), allows people to change their perception, their perspective of the circumstances and the people involved. Focusing on the positive allows them to value what they're not. PULSE conversation leaders are expected to be appreciatively intelligent, to see the potential in each person and in each situation and relationship, to see 'the mighty oak in the acorn', to take an appreciative stance and see what's good about it, to identify in a positive frame the circumstance, the significance, the possibilities and the plan.

Appreciative Inquiry provides a stance or perspective from where the circumstances can be seen differently. Like people on the sidewalk looking up, PULSE practitioners invite everyone else to look up with them, not with words so much as actions. Just by fixing their gaze on the positive aspects of the situation, they can create an environment where people move alongside and begin to look up with them to see what they see and, having seen it, move towards it in a deliberate thoughtful way.

Babs Hoffman's quote at the top of this journal page says the same thing. It is an invitation to focus on the positive and by switching focus to switch the experience. She says, "Stop worrying about the potholes in the road and enjoy the journey". *The Power of Focus*, *The Secret* and many other titles on shelves in book stores today talk about how a simple change in perspective can change our experience. The PULSE frame provides the 'how to' or crib notes for creating an environment, a conversation where that can happen. It begins with asking the positive questions, listening for the response, reframing the response to the positive, recording and confirming the reframe and moving to the next question.

***The Free Choice Principle.*** Another aspect of what underlies the PULSE frame and gives it its strength, and a principle of the study of Appreciative Inquiry is the idea that freedom of choice liberates power. It is also reflected in the work of William Glasser and choice theory. Glasser believed that giving people a sense of their own power to choose also gave them a sense of responsibility about their actions. Again and again I see evidence of this at work in conversations. When people are given the option to engage or not they engage. When they are forced to engage, they tend to disengage. Giving them the right to choose frees them to take control and ownership of both the circumstance and the resolution.

## The PULSE Pre-Meeting
Another distinguishing feature of the PULSE method for conversation is the inclusion of a pre-meeting in

the first element, Prepare, of the PULSE frame. When high emotional response, high stakes, tricky processes, controversial content or conflict are present a pre-meeting may be necessary to coach parties to speak and listen to each other differently and to inform them of the purpose, protocol and processes of the actual meeting beforehand. These meetings are held individually with each of the parties. The PULSE frame employs the individual caucus type meeting to accomplish a number of things. The first is to establish rapport with the parties and the neural link that is necessary if they are to trust the PULSE practitioner and the PULSE process. In the pre-meeting, PULSE practitioners have the opportunity to introduce the process, set the protocol and, explain why it works. They have an opportunity to hear the story and to begin to reframe it while the other party is not present. Allowing parties to share their story in the pre-meeting allows for the catharsis that is so necessary for people to be psychologically prepared to move on. It allows parties to test the impartiality of the PULSE practitioner and they do. It provides them with information so that they know what will happen in the actual meeting. In fact, knowing what will happen allows them to more readily contribute and co-construct reality in the next meeting. When they know what should happen, they make sure it does. This is the Anticipatory Principle at work.

The pre-meeting is set up in a deliberate way to have parties consider the circumstance from a different perspective, again reflecting Appreciative Inquiry principles. The questions that are asked in the pre-meeting engage parties in a reconsideration of the events, the story, their own perception of the present situation and the possibilities for a future together. The key question in the pre-meeting is the miracle question. "If a miracle happened and this were resolved how would you know?" The question is adapted from Brief Solution Focused Therapy. It forces the parties to imagine a future where all their needs are met. Often they know what's not good about the situation but they have not considered what "good" would actually look like. The miracle question provides the opportunity to think about it. The scaling questions are also helpful. They include, "Where are you now on a scale of one to ten, ten being the miracle?" "Are there times when the miracle has already happened?" and "What would it take to move one step closer to the miracle?" These questions invite parties to see the possibilities and become hopeful.

The pre-meeting is very much a coaching session where participants are preparing for game day or the actual meeting. The rules of the game are explained, the expectations are made clear, the control of the circumstances defined and the significance of the conversation and the priority of the resolution are acknowledged. The credibility and authority of the referee or PULSE practitioner are also established in the pre-meeting. Skillful PULSE practitioners can differentiate themselves from the party and the situation. They are emotionally mature. Bowen Theory holds that the ability to differentiate is a key element of emotional maturity which is defined as the ability to manage emotional situations. PULSE practitioners need to be able to differentiate, distance, objectify, or what PULSE practitioners call detach, from the circumstance so that they can 'go to the balcony' (Fisher and Ury 1992), a phrase used by Ury and Fisher to explain this kind of objectifying or distancing by the mediator.

Following the PULSE frame and the script which is written in a way so as to ensure detachment and differentiation, PULSE practitioners can create the neural link or connection with the parties individually. The neural link is also defined by Bowen as key to emotional maturity. Looking at the speaker, providing eye contact, understanding without agreement, are all skills used and modeled by PULSE practitioners in the PULSE frame.

This initially is done individually during the pre-meeting so that any danger of misinterpretation or defensiveness on the part of the other parties is mitigated. Some mediators or conversation leaders like to hear the stories and coach the parties on the protocol for the conversation with all parties present. The PULSE frame does that in the Prepare stage of the actual meeting, repeating the information from the pre-meeting when the parties are together. The purpose of the repetition is to ensure they have confidence that they have all heard the same information in the pre-meeting and that the PULSE practitioner is credible, and trustworthy. Once they hear the information repeated, they gain confidence in the PULSE practitioner and they understand that there will be no surprises with the process. This repetition is deliberate. Together they confirmed the purpose, process, protocol, authority, confidentiality and timeframe for the conversation and begin to understand their role. Their first introduction to all of that happens separately so that they can feel confident asking questions without losing face and so that they can actually hear what is being said without the emotional layer of sitting across from other parties.

The first ten minutes of any highly emotional meeting is always about calming people, relaxing them so that they can think. Repeating what they already know, having them acknowledge and agree to ground rules they have already heard and timelines they are aware of, is a very effective technique. Another way to create a safe environment for the conversation is to establish, clearly, who is in charge of the process. This is also a calming technique. Tensions arise with humans and with animals when they don't know who is in charge. The PULSE practitioner, having established rapport, connection and the neural link in the pre-meeting, moves into the actual meeting with a confident 'I-am-in-charge-of-the-process-and-you-will-find-a-resolution' approach that given the anticipatory principle defines the conversation before it even begins.

* * *

Ralph Waldo Emerson has just chimed in from the top of the page. "The world is all gates, all opportunities, strings of tension waiting to be struck." The gates and opportunities can be found in the conversations. They are strings of tension, unresolved conflicts, that when struck with the physiological and psychological deliberateness of the PULSE frame and practitioner, create music and harmony rather than simple noise. The physiological and psychological deliberateness of the PULSE frame gives it its elegance and its strength. It separates it from other conversation structures and contributes to its continued success.

In summary, the *Learn* chapter was about learning the significance of PULSE, what makes the discovery of the conversation frame important. PULSE is important because it takes a staged conversation from the field of mediation, accepts that the stages of the conversation are fluid and not static, defines the purpose of each stage in terms of the principles of

Appreciative Inquiry, incorporates understandings of human behavior from the Enneagram *and* holds people capable of resolving their own disputes and making their own decisions. It is this last distinction that provides the insightful difference. PULSE practitioners hold parties capable. They believe in people and in their ability to co-construct a better future. They have faith in the people and the process that will guide them. Five simple questions make the difference; how will we speak and listen to each other; what needs to be resolved; why is it important; what could be done; and what will be done.

Prepare for the conversation

Uncover the circumstance

Learn the significance

Search the possibilities

Explain a plan of action

Using the BEACH acronym as a guide to summarize this chapter it is easy to see that the PULSE frame demonstrates a Belief in the individual to resolve their own issues, an Expectation that people will grow toward what nourishes them, an Assumption that positive questions will lead to positive answers and futures, a Concern that without detachment practitioners will do more harm than good and a Hope that we can create world peace one conversation at the time.

Frank Lloyd Wright said "Tip the world over on its side and everything that is loose will land in Los Angeles." I would add "Distill any successful conversation and you will find evidence of the PULSE process, the PULSE stance and PULSE theory." PULSE is a discovery, not an invention, and evidence of the elements of the theory can be found everywhere. It includes all that is 'loose' in the study of conversation. It is unique in its combination of thoughts, theories and approaches. It is elegant in its comprehensiveness and consistency and it is important to relationships and organizations in a world searching for conversations.

# Chapter 4: Search the Possibilities

This chapter sets out to explore possibilities for the application of the PULSE frame. Over the past five years it has proven itself as a peacemaking tool for resolving disputes of any and all kinds. When the PULSE frame is used in everyday life it has the potential to allow people to avoid the need for its use in high conflict situations by mitigating the occurrences of unresolved conflict. PULSE conversations are a core competency for leaders and organizations and mediators in the field. The structure and the principles remain the same in any and all situations. The variables include the number of parties, complexity of the situation and the purpose for which the frame is being used. An unintended impact of the PULSE frame is to reduce stress in the workplace and to allow for the creation of relationships that are fulfilling and a workforce that is sustainable.

There are many ways to apply PULSE. When I began to look for ways to apply the frame I felt like Paul Theroux who said "I sought trains; I found passengers." People who have used PULSE and who have become PULSE practitioners share with us again and again the many ways this not so 'secret' weapon has worked for them. Each of the possible applications of PULSE, are explained in greater detail in this chapter. Others may emerge. We welcome your insight as you too experience other ways that the PULSE frame can be applied.

## PULSE as a Writing Tool

I used PULSE to organize and structure this book. The titles of the chapters reflect the frame and it serves to organize each of the chapters and the thoughts that I had hoped to communicate as the story is told. In the past I have used the PULSE frame to structure the writing of my dissertation on Accountability and Change. I have used it to write emails, articles and newsletters. As an organizing structure for any kind of writing it is a handy tool. Writing answers to the PULSE questions is a very effective way of preparing people for the piece with the opening paragraph; uncovering the past circumstance; learning the present significance; searching the possible future and explaining the conclusion, the plan of action: Prepare, Uncover, Learn, Search and Explain.

## PULSE for Training

The structure is also used to organize training workshops. Five day workshops devote one day per element. The first day is dedicated to *preparing* people for the learning. The second day is *uncovering* from the participants and trainer what is already known. The third day is an opportunity for participants to *learn* from each other in experiential situations, the significance of the learning. The fourth day is about *searching* applications for the new learning and the fifth day is *explaining* in writing how the learning will be integrated back into the workplace. Even a one day workshop will prepare participants by describing the process, protocol, purpose, authority, confidentiality and time frame. Then what is known from the past will be uncovered. The goods are delivered in Uncover. It is where the skills and concepts are taught. Participants learn the significance of the learning from each other in an experiential setting, engaging in dialogue to explore what's important about the learning. Then they search applications for the learning and explain in writing a plan of action for what they will do differently as a result of the experiences. Each of the questions goes to a different purpose and learning. Prepare answers the question 'how' and describes the means by which participants will acquire the new knowledge. Uncover answers the question 'what' and reveals the mystery of what is already known, providing new information for consideration. Learn answers the question 'why' and reveals the meaning of the learning ... what is important. Search asks 'what if' and explores the methods that can be used to apply the learning. Explain asks 'what's next' or 'so what'. It reveals the plan of action, the map or the means for moving forward and integrating the knowledge into present practice so that participants become PULSE practitioners. In fact it becomes clearer as participants move through the learning process that Explain leads back into the next PULSE, the next learning opportunity. In terms of structuring learning, PULSE is used to prepare means, uncover mystery, learn meaning, search methods and explain means again.

# PULSE as a Planning Tool

PULSE is also a planning tool. As a strategic planning tool it has its roots in the Canadian forces battle planning procedures and can be used to plan and execute any kind of event. At the PULSE Institute we have worked with project managers to integrate the concepts into their work so that they can avoid distractions and delays by being proactive in planning conversations. The PULSE frame is applied to the project to plan it and the frame also guides the conversations that introduce the plan and execute the plan. It is used to organize meetings and interface with contractors. There are PULSE's within PULSE's.

In Prepare, the purpose of the project is made clear to everyone in a face-to-face meeting. The protocol for dealing with members of the team and clients and contractors is established. Clauses may even be written into partnering agreements that require a mediated PULSE conversation as a first step in resolving conflict or tension between the parties. Process is explained in detail and posters which outline the PULSE frame are distributed. Authority and confidentiality are addressed and clearly understood and a process for asking questions about either is established. Timelines are outlined. Prepare may be a series of meetings or a one day partnering meeting. The one day partnering or team building event uses the PULSE frame as an organizer so that the parties can experience the frame while they learn about it. Parties should also have an opportunity to meet individually with a project manager in the pre-meeting so that the project manager can establish the rapport, the authority he or she will need to manage the project effectively.

In Uncover, it becomes very clear what the event or project is. This is often defined by the client. The PULSE practitioner will ensure the clarity that is necessary to create a successful outcome. Ensuring that parties answer the question "What are you here to plan, decide or resolve with this project?" in a one word title is the PULSE practitioner's job. To accomplish that, the practitioner will ask everyone individually to answer the question, speaking directly to them, while the others are present. From everyone's story they pull the one word title for the combined story. "So you are here to plan health care for kids" or "You are here to plan a hospital". Using the parties' words is important and having everyone agree to the title of the project is also important. Even if the answer is obvious, asking it and having everyone agree again on what it is they're doing as a team builds purpose and a sense of working together. Nodding together at the beginning of a project saves a lot of grief later on.

In Learn, the PULSE practitioner listens for criteria that will make the plan or project successful. Identifying what's important to people individually and as a group creates understanding and awareness. Different groups have different criteria, and that is expected. Sharing the criteria, the individual or unique and the common, helps everyone understand what needs to happen. Identifying the criteria for success allows people to work together in a way that acknowledges their different and their shared goals. Sometimes the unique criteria are buried in defensive language so project managers or PULSE practitioners have to know how to reframe, to find out what's missing for people and name it in a positive, appreciative way that values participants and their contribution. Knowledge of the Enneagram is very helpful in this kind of exercise. The

Enneagram teaches the basic human motivations, the things that maybe missing or the different criteria people have for measuring success.

Once the criteria have been identified the Search stage in PULSE planning asks participants to brainstorm possibilities and to test those ideas or options against the unique and common criteria. Together parties decide which are feasible and doable and within their authority; which options will contribute to the success of the project or event. In Explain, the plan is revealed by having parties contribute the wording and the details of how things will be done.  It is in Explain where practitioners work with parties to get agreement on who will do what by when.

The PULSE Planning Conversation is PULSE's within PULSE's.  Each stage requires PULSE meetings and conversations. It is like a kaleidoscope where all the pieces are always the same but where a twist or change in perspective reveals a new and different configuration, a reorganization of the same information. An infinite number of PULSE conversations combine to make a PULSE Project Planning guide that is effective at improving the quality of the conversations and meetings and the relationships that are the medium for the work within the project.  Improving the quality of the conversation improves the quality of the project.  As Joyce Carol Oates said, at the top of this journal page, "It's where we go, and what we do when we get there, that tells us who we are."  The PULSE planning tool helps us insure that we go and do what we intend to do and do not get sidetracked or stray too far from who we want to be.

# PULSE Negotiation

Earlier this week I heard Bill Ury speak at a conference. He was talking about when and how to say no, the importance of saying no in a way that people can hear it. Parties are encouraged in the PULSE frame to speak gently to each other; to be honest; and say what they're thinking even if it is 'no'; to be open to hearing the other person's story and allowing that story to influence perceptions of the circumstance; to use specific examples for clarity; and talk to each other and find a gentle way to share what they're thinking. The GHOST protocol (gentle, honest, open, specific, talk) encourages people to speak so the other person can keep on listening and I think that is what Bill Ury was talking about. He was defining a gentle way to say no. Ury and Fisher's *Getting to Yes* is very widely read in the field of negotiation. The way I see it, the PULSE frame offers a simple yet effective structure for doing just that … getting to yes. When PULSE is used as a negotiation tool, one of the P's on the left of the chart disappears. The delta still represents the PULSE practitioner, someone who has a desire to improve or change conversations and relationships, whatever their official title or position may be. The delta still does most of the talking in Prepare, getting agreement from the other on the purpose, process, protocol, authority, confidentiality, and time. In Uncover, each party individually answers the question "What are we here to resolve today?" and the delta manages the naming of the common story in a brief, neutral title. Then both parties learn directly from each other in a dialogue about why the circumstances are important to them and the delta records and summarizes these unique and common criteria. Once criteria are set, parties search possibilities in a brainstorm together. The delta captures the ideas on the chart paper. Then parties evaluate their options against the criteria deciding which are feasible and doable and within their authority. Once options are identified, they sit together and the delta acts as scribe to explain in writing a plan of action to guide their future together.

PULSE negotiation is efficient and effective. Negotiations that once might have taken two or three days can be reduced to one half day ... in fact 90 minutes of meeting because the 'road is paved', the 'stage is set': the work is done beforehand. There are no potholes to fall into using the PULSE frame because it clarifies for everyone the purpose and the process. The guiding questions serve to make each stage intentional and deliberate. Skilled practitioners structure the negotiating conversation so that any one issue can be negotiated to mutually satisfactory result in about one to one and a half hours. I have seen it work again and again even in multiple party negotiations were facilitators are used to manage the PULSE process and guide the negotiation. One hour and a half to resolve longstanding issues ... like magic. Glenn Clark's quote at the top of this page says "If you wish to travel far and fast, travel light." All you need to manage a negotiation is the PULSE frame. Follow the process and let it work. It will help you travel far and fast, resolving even difficult issues quickly and with resolutions that may not have seemed possible before the PULSE conversation began. He continues "Take off all your envies, jealousies, unforgiveness, selfishness and fears." Step into the circle of resolution with a willingness to resolve and an appreciative, empathetic stance and watch the magic begin.

The PULSE frame can also be used to interview a client when you are asked to negotiate on behalf of someone else. To be effective as a negotiator you will need to understand what the client wants negotiated (Uncover), what is important to them (Learn) and what options they would consider (Search). By taking them through the PULSE negotiation frame, including the frame of the pre-meeting which includes the miracle question, you are fully prepared to represent the client or customer or union member in the actual PULSE negotiated meeting.

## PULSE Mediation

When there is anger, there is conflict and some conflicts need the intervention of a professional. The PULSE frame evolved from the five stage models of mediation like the one Cheryl Picard presents in her book *Mediating Small Group and Interpersonal Disputes.* It has been tested as a mediation tool in civil claims, community mediation and in private practice countless times with excellent results. As a mediation frame it continues to be successful bringing parties to settlement in the solution, and building and maintaining sustainable relationships. The PULSE frame that has evolved, incorporates not only the five stages of the Picard model but the Appreciative Inquiry stance and the physiological and psychological findings of Dan Dana and the understanding of participants that comes with the study of the Enneagram.

PULSE has been used in co-mediation, civil claims, community mediations, multiparty mediation, oil company to oil company disputes, and many workplace and family disputes. In a PULSE mediation the mediators or practitioners meet with the party separately first in a pre-meeting where they introduce the process, protocol, and purpose of the mediation and outline expectations around authority, confidentiality and time and gain a commitment from the parties to the process. In a formal, third party intervention or mediation this commitment is in writing. In the pre-meeting the mediators establish rapport and create the neural link, the connection necessary for participants to trust the mediator and the process. The mediator leads an Appreciative Inquiry into the communication the parties have shared to date, asking parties to talk about the good conversations and preparing the parties to speak and listen to each other differently. Parties are asked to speak in a gentle rather than respectful way because out of respect sometimes things are left unsaid. This may hinder the process rather than contribute to a satisfactory resolution. In a PULSE conversation or mediation parties are encouraged to speak so the other person can keep on listening, to say what's on their mind, to be honest, in a gentle way. Parties are encouraged to be open to hearing what the other parties are saying, understanding that they have been asked to speak gently as well. Parties are asked to listen for new information and allow what is being said to influence their perceptions. Parties are asked to use specific examples, to bring clarity and a common understanding of the circumstances and they are also asked to stay in the conversation until a balanced, mutually agreeable resolution can be reached. It is made clear that the mediator leads the process and the parties will resolve the dispute. Ownership of the outcome is key to sustaining the relationship. At the end of the pre-meeting, a decision is made to use PULSE mediated conversations or to explore other methods of dispute resolution.

"A good traveler has no fixed plans and is not intent on arriving" Lao-Tzu adds from the top of the page. PULSE mediators have no vested interest in the outcome and will go where participants take then. The PULSE mediator follows the parties as they move through the mediated conversation gently guiding them through the questions: asking, listening, capturing, summarizing, confirming, and moving to the next question. Once the process is described to the parties in the pre-meeting and then again in Prepare in the actual mediation, it flows as it has been described, just as the Anticipatory Principle tells us it will.

In Prepare, the mediator outlines the process again using the PULSE poster as a visual guide. The protocol and the purpose are also outlined once again for clarity. The mediator confirms authority, confidentiality and time and describes the roles of the mediator and the parties and confirms a willingness to proceed. A "Consent to Mediate or Participate" is signed at the end of Prepare to confirm the party's commitment to the process of mediation, and at a deeper level, to the importance of the relationship. The consent form is signed in front of the other party so that each of them understands the commitment of the other to the process and the relationship and so that they can begin to connect. The connection and commitment will lead them to a mutually agreeable resolution.

In Uncover, parties speak directly to the mediator individually to answer the question "What are you here to resolve today?" The mediator thanks each party after they speak being careful to look at the speaker, giving full attention and yet remaining impartial or detached. Once both parties have spoken the mediator names the story ... not one story or the other ... but the thing that both parties are talking about, the circumstance that needs to be resolved. Once named, the mediator writes the one-word neutral title on the chart paper, and confirms by asking "If this circumstance could be resolved would that be time well spent?"

In Learn, the mediator reminds the parties of the GHOST protocol and then asks them to speak directly to each other and answer the question "What about the circumstances is important to you?" The mediator looks at the listener to encourage direct communication between the parties. The mediator listens for and records the criteria for resolution identified in the conversation, the beliefs, expectations, assumptions, concerns, and hopes that the parties reveal as they talk to each other. When a conciliatory gesture goes unnoticed, the mediator may ask the speaker to say more about that. The goal is to kick start the move to the Green Zone by changing perceptions using a reframe, stating things in a positive way and identifying what's missing for the parties. The mediator suggests and records two unique criteria for each of the parties and two common criteria. The PULSE mediator uses the knowledge of the Enneagram to hunch what the unique and often competing criteria might be. The Enneagram also provides insight into possible common criteria or common ground or BEACH on which to build the future. It is important for the mediator to identify both unique and common criteria. One legitimizes the dispute. The other provides hope for a better future together. The mediator records the criteria on the chart paper and posts it next to the circumstance and then moves to the brainstorming stage, Search.

In Search the mediator records ideas or options for resolution on chart paper in scattered bubbles. No priority or level of importance is given to any option. The mediator opens by stating "Given that 'something' and 'something' are important to you and 'something else' and 'something else' are important to you and that for both of you 'something else again' and 'something else again' are important, your opportunity now is to generate options that will meet your unique and common criteria and resolve your circumstance. Mediation works best when there are ten to twelve ideas to work with.  What could you do to resolve the circumstance and meet your criteria?" Once ten to twelve verbs phrases have been captured in the random bubbles on the chart the mediator, who has remained silent while capturing the ideas, takes a different color pen and circles the options that both parties agree are feasible, doable and within their authority.

In Explain, the mediator acts as scribe and writes the plan using the words of the parties, recording what the parties agreed to do.  The plan is reviewed and commitment to the ideas in the plan of action is checked and double checked to ensure that it is well understood and sustainable.  Then the mediator reviews the purpose, the process, the protocol, the authority, the confidentiality, and the time, thanks the parties for coming and encourages them to use the process of PULSE, Prepare, Uncover, Learn, Search and Explain and the gentle, honest, open, specific talk protocol to resolve other differences that may arise between them.

The PULSE mediator remains impartial, detached from the outcome, and yet connected to the parties, as they guide participants to reconsider and reframe the story from the past, the impact of the present, and the risks for the future. PULSE mediation is powerful.  Some even describe it as magical because of  the way that people who cannot even look at each other when they come into a mediation, are transformed to people with a plan to work together and play together when the leave. Key factors are the positive, appreciative stance, the impartiality, the emotional maturity of the mediator as guardian of the process. A wise native friend of mine once told me "Nancy, the chief speaks first and the chief speaks last. It's that way all over the world." That applies in mediation. The presence of a confident conversation leader who sets things up with a strong introduction and then wraps the decision and the process into a neat package at the end is critical to the success of the conversation. A mediator who acts as if the issue can be resolved by the parties, who holds them capable, will be successful every time. It is that calming effect of the 'mediator', 'the delta' or 'practitioner', the 'alpha male or female' in the animal kingdom or the 'chief' in my friend's language, that cannot be ignored.

In our workshops I hear feedback to new mediators from their role play participants that provides evidence of the significance of the role. "I knew you were there just in case and so I was calm." "You disappeared for me when we were talking together". No greater compliment can be given a mediator. What they are really saying is "You gave me the confidence to handle my own stuff." Mediators are about holding parties capable and about working themselves out of the job. There is power in the unleashing of personal power, through choice. Empowering participants and holding them accountable and capable for resolving their own issue is counter-intuitive and it works. PULSE mediators not only guide parties to resolution, they also give them the tools for dealing with each other differently in the future than they have in the past.

PULSE mediators believe as Walt Whitman says at the top of this page, "Not I - not anyone else, can travel that road for you. You must travel it for yourself."

PULSE mediators and practitioners believe in the psychology of personal power advocated by William Glasser. No one other than the parties can travel the road to resolution. They have to do it for themselves. The PULSE practitioner is the guide, providing a map and directions towards resolution. Parties choose for themselves whether or not they will accept the guidance.

## PULSE Appreciative Inquiry: Change Management

Another application of the PULSE frame is a structure for Appreciative Inquiry. Appreciative Inquiry is a tool used in organizational development that focuses questions and responses on the positive aspects of an organization to promote positive change. It has been very successful in changing cultures with its positive, appreciative approach. It is a process with defined stages that are consistent with the Prepare, Uncover, Learn, Search, Explain steps. Rather than use a different frame for this kind of inquiry it seemed to me that using the same frame for the conversations *and* the management of the change initiative would make sense. In PULSE AI, the delta represents the agent for change, the practitioner leading the change. The literature on AI describes a four stage process: the four D's of Discovery, Dream, Design, and Deliver. Before the four D's there are steps aimed at selecting a method for inquiry and identifying the affirmative topic. In the PULSE AI frame, Prepare is where the methods for inquiry are determined and shared. The purpose, the process, and the protocol are established along with authority, confidentiality, time and the roles that people will play in the inquiry. The PULSE Uncover is where the affirmative topic is identified using the same flow of conversation as in other applications of the frame, asking for each individual's answer to the question "What you are here to inquire into today?" The size of group in Uncover may be a smaller than the entire organization depending on decisions made in Prepare. Once the circumstance of the inquiry has been identified in Uncover, then the work of learning the criteria for change begins. In AI it is referred to as Discovering the positive core. In PULSE it is called Learn. In both instances it is a dialogue about what's working. In PULSE Learn the practitioner uses the question "What about this is important to you?" to begin to gather the beliefs, expectations, assumptions, concerns, and hopes that will form the criteria for a sustainable, mutually agreeable, resolution or change...the positive core.

In the PULSE Search phase parties brainstorm options to meet their criteria. In AI the equivalent would be the Dream piece, which in some ways looks similar to the miracle question of the pre-meeting mentioned earlier. PULSE uses the miracle question to have parties begin to think about the possible futures. The Dream piece from AI is also aimed at identifying what could be. The question from PULSE is "What could you do?" as possibilities for a different future are explored.

Explain, in PULSE AI asks "What do you agree to do?". The PULSE practitioner captures the plan in writing. The PULSE AI plans are a series of provocative propositions. In AI Provocative Propositions are used to describe the future as if it were already true. These are written in active voice and present tense to add strength to participants' commitment. In AI this occurs in the Design piece, which is followed by the Delivery piece in AI, and the second E in PULSE: Prepare, Uncover, Search, Explain, Execute the plan. The follow-up in the PULSE AI takes the form of another PULSE using the PULSE planning structure from PULSE Project Management.

Kelm (2005) defines Appreciative Inquiry as

- a positive strength-based approach to change
- finding the best in people in the world around them
- co-creating inspiring future images
- focusing on what we want more of
- finding and unleashing the positive core (page 180)


My provocative proposition is that PULSE is AI for relationships. PULSE also provides a structure for the AI conversation. The PULSE within PULSE's idea provides the means. The PULSE conversation frame can be used for every conversation with an AI. It is consistent with the principles. It is a positive, strength and confidence-based approach to conversations and change. It focuses on the positive, and what parties want more of. It enables parties to co-create inspiring futures by identifying and unleashing the positive core, the criteria for resolution and a sustainable relationship.


## Changing Routines with PULSE

"I love to sail forbidden seas, and land on barbarous coasts." Herman Melville may have been talking about the seas but for me the sailing I love to do is to explore forbidden 'seas', to uncover what Noonan (2007) calls the 'undiscussables', the barbarous coasts, where the 'barbarians' live. In every workplace there are barbarians, at least in the minds of coworkers. Chris

Argyris identified what he called *defensive routines* in workplaces that are destructive and counterproductive. Changing the routines has proven difficult. Evidence of unresolved conflict and unchanging defensive routines exist in almost every organization. The PULSE frame provides a structure for doing just that. Argyris identified two strategies himself that have become widely accepted in businesses and in organizational development: the Ladder of Inference discussed in Chapter 3 and the left hand column, the LHC, where people write what they are thinking, writing the things they don't want to say in a meeting or conversation and then share that with others when they can find a way to say it.

In the PULSE frame, the practitioner encourages parties to say what they're thinking in a gentle way. Gentle means speaking in a way that allows the other parties to keep on listening, a way that will not bring up defenses. PULSE uses gentle rather than respectful because of the danger of having information withheld out of respect or fear which Argyris describes as the beginning of the defense of routine. Parties are informed that withholding information is counterproductive. "Say what you're thinking" is the mantra of the PULSE practitioner. Astronauts are trained to do just that because their thoughts, no matter how trivial, contribute to the success of the mission. The same is true of participants in PULSE conversations. Full disclosure and saying what you're thinking is critical and crucial. Finding a gentle way to do it is key, a way that allows what you are saying to be heard.

Simply encouraging co-workers to speak gently to each other may change the routines away from defensiveness. Participants seem to understand how to say things so that buttons are not pushed.  They understand "gentle" as soft but truthful, firm but friendly.  Honesty plays an important role too, in the way that parties of PULSE conversations are encouraged to speak.  Some of the issues with the training and Argyris's LHC work arose because people got suspicious and believed that things were being withheld.  People felt that others were being less than honest with each other.  The other problem was that some people used the LHC opportunity to be honest in a less than gentle way, to beat up on or become verbally aggressive with their fellow workers.  A gentle, honest, open, specific, talk protocol that encourages people to say what they are thinking in a gentle way, such as that offered in the PULSE conversation, achieves what the LHC exercise set out to do.  The GHOST protocol from the PULSE frame does it in a more effective and satisfying way.  Parties are held to a standard of communication that mitigates defensiveness and allows for positive, productive, gentle, honest, open, specific, talk.  People now have a strategy for avoiding the defensive routines that have kept them stuck and can move toward a more productive and positive future together.

The PULSE frame and the PULSE delta, or practitioner, use questions to back people down the Ladder of Inference to the observable data.  Using PULSE, beliefs and assumptions are identified as criteria for resolution.  Perceptions of the situation are reframed and expanded.  PULSE is a structure for the double loop thinking that Argyris talks about and the deeper U learning in *Presence: An Exploration of Profound Change in People, Organizations, and Society*, another book on the subject by Senge et al.  The use of the PULSE frame slows people down and asks them to consider and reconsider the past story in Uncover, the present impact in Learn, the future possibilities in Search, and to come to a plan of action for the future in Explain. This new approach to conversation changes the defensive routines and provides people with the structure they need to have the difficult conversations and discuss the 'undiscussables'.

## PULSE Coaching

As a frame for a coaching conversation, PULSE has many advantages. First of all it holds the participant or client capable of resolving their own situation. It builds on the strength and knowledge of the individual, not the coach. It covers the past circumstance, the present impact and criteria for better futures and the possibilities for futures as well. Guiding people to their own conclusions is the ultimate aim of personal and professional coaching. PULSE does that. It provides purpose, process and protocol. It considers confidentiality, authority to act and time. Coaching clients to use the PULSE frame to structure difficult, crucial or dangerous conversations empowers them to deal with situations and circumstances differently.

## PULSE Facilitation

PULSE Facilitation is PULSE Mediation with more people in the room. The process remains the same. The intent of each of the phases remains the same and the outcome is sustainable, feasible and doable. Even the time frame for the facilitated conversation remains a ninety minute frame. Each of the parties has time in a pre-meeting before the PULSE Conversation to meet with the delta or practitioner to learn about the process and begin to identify the circumstance, criteria for resolution and possible futures. Groups of people representing similar criteria for resolution or interests may meet with the PULSE facilitator together to clarify their approach to the conversation and to establish rapport with the facilitator.

## PULSE Meetings

Any meeting will benefit from the use of the PULSE frame to structure the conversation. It provides the road map that ensures that all aspects for consideration are surfaced. Think about meetings you have attended where the circumstance or decision that needed to be made was unclear. How might the PULSE frame have improved such a meeting? Think about a meeting where solutions are considered before *criteria* for solutions are identified. Outcomes from these meetings usually meet the needs of some people in the room but not others. The likelihood of their sustainable success is compromised, as not everyone is satisfied with the outcome, or it does not work to meet their needs. Think of meetings that jump right to solutions and a plan of action. What is missing in those meetings is a consideration of the past and the present, a consideration of the contributions of the people in the room. The emotional and physical aspects of the circumstances are not taken into account.

By contrast a PULSE meeting moves deliberately from Prepare or "How will this meeting proceed?" to Uncover or "What is this meeting about?" to Learn or "Why is the topic important?" to Search or "What can we do?" and Explain or "What will we do?" Everyone leaves the meeting knowing what the next steps will be. The topic, the criteria, the options and the plan are clear.

## PULSE Self-Talk

Even when you are sorting our something for yourself, using the PULSE frame to organize your thoughts can be useful.  When you are listening to someone else, ask yourself "What are they talking about?" and "Why it is important to them?".  Doing this puts you in a position where you can identify the motivation of others, where you can put yourself in their position, where you can empathize in the sense of seeing the world from their perspective.  This kind of self-talk, even when it is about your own circumstance or criteria  will allow for more deliberate, well constructed answers to questions from others in difficult situations.  Using the frame slows the conversation and the thinking down enough that you can be confident in your reply.

## PULSE Leadership

*The Harvard Business Review* recently published an article by Dave Ulrich and Norm Smallwood which outlines five principles for building leadership capacity.  The first principle that they identify is "Nail the prerequisites of leadership" and they outline a five-point protocol.  In the PULSE frame, Prepare is about identifying the prerequisites for the conversation and it outlines a five point protocol: gentle, honest, open , specific talk.  The second principle identified by Ulrich and Smallwood is "Connect your executives' abilities to the reputation you are trying to establish."  PULSE's Uncover answers the question 'what?' In the case of building a leadership brand, as Ulrich and Smallwood suggest, it is about making a clear statement about what leadership is.  The third principle identified in the article is "Assess leaders against the statement of leadership brand." The authors suggest feedback sessions with customers and other kinds of dialogue consistent with Learn in PULSE where parties learn from each other the significance of the situation. The fourth principle is "Let the customers and investors do the teaching." This principle suggests that there are options to consider for meeting the requirements or criteria as there are in the PULSE Search where the "What if?" question is addressed. The fifth principle "Track the long term success of your leadership brand efforts", relates to the Explain of the PULSE frame, looking to answer the question "What's next?" Principles and processes come in fives ... Prepare, Uncover, Learn, Search, and Explain.

PULSE Leadership is about being a conversation leader. In my dissertation work, I studied five leaders, leading mandated change. The conversations were the key. They are the medium through which leaders do their work. Leaders negotiated perceptions of the mandated change through many different types of conversations. To be successful it was important to at least touch on three points. First, the followers in my study needed to understand that they had had some influence or control over the introduction of the mandated change. The greater the perception of control the more likely the followers were to accept responsibility and change their behaviours. Second, they needed to understand that the change initiative was a priority. Thirdly they needed to have clear perceptions of the expectations for the change in behaviour for them.

PULSE leaders are skilled in the art and the science of the conversations that lead to change through the acceptance of responsibility for change among their followers. If responsibility is not accepted, or if the behaviour deviates from what is expected because of the change, then the conversation between leader and follower changes to one of accountability. Now the conversation is about compliance. Again, the leader needs to negotiate perceptions of how non-compliance has been handled in the past, the importance of the approval of the leader and the risk of non-compliance. I found that leaders had both types of conversations: responsibility and accountability. They negotiated past circumstances, present significance and future expectations in both conversations.

Because of the significance of conversation and other kinds of communication in leadership, it has become apparent to me that the use of the PULSE frame improves the effectiveness of leaders. It is a core competency for dealing with meetings, with conflict, with planning, with administration of any kind. It allows leaders to be more effective with clients, employees and bosses. It provides a means by which to use the medium of conversation to advantage and to lead people as well as to manage the relationships with them.

The significance of conversation as a medium through which leadership is accomplished is best understood when leadership is redefined as Vicarious Responsibility. Leaders only experience what their followers do vicariously, through conversation, and they only influence the outcome of their followers vicariously, through conversation... But a full PULSE exploration of that topic will have to wait for another book.

\* \* \*

Florence Prag Kahn said "Travel not only stirs the blood … it also gives strength to the spirit." Strengthening the spirit, the GHOST in PULSE, is important. Travel through the PULSE frame strengthens communication skills, stirring the blood and strengthening the spirit. It creates hope: hope for a future together that is better than the past, bringing forward what is good from the past relationship, shining a light on it, nourishing it in an appreciative way. People, like plants, grow toward what nourishes them. Focusing on the positive generates more positiveness and hopefulness in people, in relationships, in conversations and in organizations. PULSE is a means to this end. PULSE communication is appreciative, encouraging, empowering, and yet it holds people accountable. PULSE increases the flow of good, positive information. PULSE pushes information, the life blood...vitality, and gives strenth and vitality to conversation and relationship.

# Chapter 5: Explain a Plan of Action

Given that there are many possibilities for the application of the PULSE Conversation frame; given that it can be used to write, to teach, to plan, to manage projects, to negotiate, to mediate, to lead Appreciative Inquiries, to dissolve defensive routines, to frame any conversation, to lead effectively; given that it is unique in its combination of the principles of Appreciative Inquiry, the emotional maturity that comes with a study of the Enneagram, the physiological and psychological science of conversation; and that it is a way of feeling, doing and thinking, a way of moving people from the past, to the present and on to a hopeful future, what are the next steps for PULSE?  This chapter sets out to do what Explain in the frame does ... to outline in detail what next - to answer the questions who, what, where, when, and how and to remove any obstacles to the satisfactory completion of this plan.  It takes the form of a call to action and a commitment on my part and the part of PULSE to continue to honour and promote the frame as a means to peaceful, productive ends.

First of all PULSE is committed to continuing with education and training.  Today, more than 500 PULSE practitioners are out there in organizations and families changing how people feel, what they do, and how they think about conversations. PULSE will continue the use of the frame for learning conversations all over the world.  In fact it has become our primary goal to teach people how to use the PULSE frame in all of the ways that it can be used. Given that the attitude, skills and knowledge of the PULSE frame is a core competency for leadership in any organization, it is our intention to teach and train 1000 PULSE practitioners over the next year.  PULSE and I are also committed to using the frame to write articles and newsletters, new programs of study and books so that others will learn about PULSE. We are committed to supporting in what ever ways we can, the practitioners all over North America and in Africa. We're also committed to learning from others and working with others to further the use of the PULSE frame. I personally intend to speak to 2000 people at conferences or through media over the next year to introduce them to the PULSE frame

The PULSE Institute continues to use the PULSE frame to plan and organize staff meetings, projects, and events. We are committed to walking the PULSE talk in our leadership, within our own organization, and in our own conversations with each other and with our clients. Our hope is that you agree to commit to visit us when you want to learn more and to invite others to do the same. We invite you to call or write with any comments, questions or ideas that you have. We hope that you will commit to using the GHOST protocol (gentle, honest, open, specific, talk) and the PULSE process (Prepare, Uncover, Learn, Search, Explain) whenever it seems appropriate and that in every conversation you think about answering the guiding questions: How will the conversation be structured? What are we or they talking about?  Why is it important?  What could we or they do?  And what will we or they do?

"If you actually look like your passport photo, you aren't well enough to travel" is the quote at the top of the page from Sir Vivian Fuchs.  This book is a passport picture of the PULSE frame. It represents the frame and aspects of it that will make it recognizable to you when you see it but it by no means does it justice. PULSE conversations are alive and vibrant and scary and exciting and satisfying and insightful in so many ways that I know I have not captured here. It is important to try it, to see it happen right before your eyes, to meet it in person.

PULSE is a discovery. It describes how successful conversations occur. So look for it in the conversations around you. Watch people set protocol, even tacitly. Watch people move from the past, to the present and on to the future in their conversations. Hear the language they use when they're stuck in the past and in their emotions and notice what happens when response is acknowledged with a simple phrase like "This is been difficult for you." Listen for what's missing for people as they complain in their daily lives and watch how their state changes when you reframe and identify their beliefs, expectations, assumptions, concerns, and hopes in the situation by saying something like "You value your privacy" or "Flexibility is important to you." Watch as options are identified to satisfy everyone's needs and criteria. Experience the satisfaction that everyone feels when they have a solid, deliberate and detailed plan of action for the future.

You'll see and recognize, as I have, PULSE in action if you look for it. You see what you're looking for. Look for the positive. Take an appreciative PULSE stance and watch as others follow your example. Speak gently with others so they can keep on listening and watch others follow your example. Speak honestly and watch others follow your example. Be open to hearing what others have to say without defensiveness and allow what you hear to influence your perspective and watch others follow your example. Use specific examples to make your points firmly but in a friendly, gentle way and watch others follow your example. Talk. Don't just think … because thinking not talking is another TLA or three letter acronym: TNT - and that's explosive and dangerous. If you follow the GHOST principles, others will too. Just notice. Watch and be amazed at how a simple change like looking for what works or what is good, changes the way people speak and listen. Take the time to consider how the conversation will proceed, what it is about, why it is important, what could be done and what will be done in each conversation and watch how it improves the outcomes of those conversations. Be curious and Courageous. Watch for Dragons. Name the elephants. Keep the friendly PULSE GHOST with you. Be aware and mindful that:

Words create worlds,

Change the words,

Change the world.

Henry Boye said "The most important trip you may take in life is meeting people halfway." With PULSE the trip to half way is well planned, simple, effective and satisfying and you do not have to make it alone. The call to action is to use the skills, the constructs, and the frame and let us know how it goes for you. Let others know too. Our goal with PULSE remains "World peace one conversation at a time" and we know that the change begins with you.

**Other PULSE Products:**

The PULSE Conversation Script and Checklist

PULSE Mediated Conversation Video

*Vicarious Responsibility - The answer to organizational questions of leadership, conversation and everything* Dr. Nancy Love

*The POWER of PULSE* - Dr. Nancy Love

Check our website for course offerings on the following topics.

PULSE Concepts
PULSE Practice
PULSE Enneagram
PULSE Train-the-Trainer
PULSE Appreciative Inquiry
PULSE Advanced Concepts
PULSE Advanced Practice

# Appendix

## Bibliography and Reading List for PULSE Conversations for Change

Barrett, Frank, and Ronald Fry. "Appreciative Inquiry in Action: The Unfolding of a Provocative Invitation." In *Appreicative Inquiry and Organization: Reports from the Field*, by Ronald Fry, Frank Barrett, Jane Seiling and Diana Whitney, 2-23. Westport: Quorum Books, 2002.

Canfield, Jack, Mark Victor Hansen & Les Hewitt. *The Power of Focus*. Deerfield Beach: Health Communications

Cooperrider, David L. and Diana Whitney. *Appreciative Inquiry: A Positive Revolution in Change*. San Fransisco: Berrett-Kroehler Publishers Inc., 2005.

Conlon, Mara. *Old World Journal*. White Plains NY: Peter Pauper Press, 2005.

Dana, Daniel. *Managing Differences*. Kansas City: MTI Publications, 2005.

-. *The Manager-as-Mediator Seminar*. Prairie Village: MTI Publications, 2002.

DeJong, Peter & Insoo Kim Berg. *Interviewing for Solutions*. Pacific Grove: Brooks/Cole Publishing Company, 1998

Fisher, R., and William Ury. *Getting to Yes (Second Edition)*. New York: Penguin Group, 1992.

Gladwell, Malcolm. *Blink: The Power of Thinking Without Thinking*. New York:Little, Brown and Company, 2005.

Glasser, William. *Choice Theory: A New Psychology of Personal Freedom*. New York: HarperCollins Publishers, 1998.

Goleman, Daniel. *Emotional Intelligence*. New York: Bantam Books, 1995.

-. *Social Intelligence*. New York: Bantam Dell, 2006. Hammond, Sue Annis. *The Thin Book of Appreciative Inquiry*. Bend: Thin Book Publishing Co., 1998.

Senge, Peter M. et al, *Presence: An Exploration of Profound Change in People, Organizations, and Society*. SOL (Society for Organizational Learning), 2004.

Juntune, Joyce, "The Early History of the American Creativity Association" http://www.amcreativityassoc.org/ ACA%20Early%20History.pdf (accessed January 18, 2008).

Kelm, Jacqueline Bascobert, *Appreciative Living: The principals of Appreciative Inquiry in Personal Life*. Wake Forest: Venet Publishers, 2005.

Love, Charlotte Nancy. *Accountability and Change: Portraits of Five High School Principals*. Doctoral Dissertation, University of Calgary:2006

Morgan-Watson, Grahame. *The Free RHETI Sampler*. 2007.http://www.enneagraminstitute.com /dis_sample_36.asp (accessed 10 01, 2007).

Picard, Cheryl A. *Mediating Interpersonal and Small Group Conflict*. Ottawa: The Golden Dog Press, 2002.

Regina, Wayne. "A Practitioner's Guide to Effective Mediation: Applying Bowen Theory to Alternative Dispute Resolution." *Association for Conflict Resoltuion Workshop*. Phoenix, 2007.

Riso, Don Richard, and Russ Hudson. *The Wisdom of the Enneagram*. New York: Bantam Books, 1999.

Ross, Rick. "The Ladder of Inference." *In The Fifth Discipline*: *The Art and Practice of the Learning*

*Organization*, by Peter Senge, 242-246. New York: Doubleday, 1994.

Shaw, Patricia. *Changing Conversations in Organizations: A Complexity Approach to Change*. London and New York: Routledge, Taylor and Francis Group, 2002

Tallon, Robert, and Mario Sikora, *Awareness to Action, The Enneagram, Emotional Intelligence and Change*. Scranton: University of Scranton Press, 2006.

Ulrich, Dave and Norm Smallwood. "Building a Leadership Brand." *The Harvard Business Review*. July 2001.

Wheatley, Margaret J. *Leadership and the New Science: Learning about Organization from an Orderly Universe*. San Francisco: Berrett-Koehler Publishers Inc.,1994.

Whitney, Diana, and Amanda Trosten-Bloom. *The Power of Appreciative Inquiry*. San Francisco: Berrett-Koehler Publishers Inc., 2003.


**Websites**
www.enneagraminstitute.com
www.enneagram-edge.com
www.internationalenneagram.org
www.appreciative.case.edu

Madeline Hunter Lesson plans:
http://template.aea267.iowapages.org/lessonplan/index.html (accessed January 18, 2008)